## Tools and Techniques to Inspire Reading Groups

# Literature Circles

**Warren Rogers & Dave Leochko**

PORTAGE &
MAIN PRESS

Portage and Main Press acknowledges the financial support of the Government of Canada through the Book Publishing Industry Development Program (BPIDP) for our publishing activities.

Printed and bound in Canada by Hignell Book Printing

02 03 04 05 06 5 4 3 2 1

**National Library of Canada Cataloguing in Publication Data**

Rogers, Warren, 1951-

   Literature circles : tools and techniques to inspire reading groups / Warren Rogers and Dave Leochko.

   Includes bibliographical references.
   ISBN 1-895411-93-9

1. Group reading. 2. Literature—Study and teaching (Primary) 3. Group work in education. I. Leochko, Dave, 1963- II. Title.

LC6631.R63 2002 371.39'5 C2002-911098-X

Book and cover design: Gallant Design Ltd.
Story illustrations: Jess Dixon

**PORTAGE & MAIN PRESS**

100-318 McDermot Avenue
Winnipeg, Manitoba, Canada  R3A 0A2
E-mail: books@portageandmainpress.com
Tel: 204.987.3500
Toll free: 1.800.667.9673
Fax: 204.947.0080
Toll free fax: 1.866.734.8477

# CONTENTS

# Part 3: Rubrics        45

# Part 4: Short Stories        63

# Part 5: Beyond Literature Circles        127

# Bibliography        140

# INTRODUCTION

# How This Book Came To Be

**A**s colleagues in an inner-city school, teaching grades five and six, we have had many opportunities to talk about teaching methodologies and our shared experiences with students.

Initially, we discussed the qualities of well-written short stories. This led to sharing writings and providing critical feedback to each other about our attempts to write fiction. We established a system for reading and reflection with which we felt comfortable sharing our opinions and turning to each other for advice and guidance. We soon realized our students would benefit from the same kinds of discussions we were having. We believe that having children engage in thoughtful discussions about stories is an important part of their development as readers. We wondered—what is the most effective way to involve our students in valuable conversations about stories?

It was at this point that Literature Circles became part of our dialogue. One of us had been working with Literature Circles for a couple of years; the other was just discovering the process. Our varied experiences allowed us to articulate and formulate our beliefs, principles, and practices about literature. As we continued to work together, we realized we had materials we could share with all teachers, regardless of their background experiences with Literature Circles. This book, a compilation of our material, has the foundations required for initial set-up; six original short stories; as well as some time-saving sheets for practitioners.

PART 1

# LITERATURE CIRCLES

# WHAT ARE LITERATURE CIRCLES?

A Literature Circle is a group of people who meets on a regular basis to discuss stories and books. The reason for getting together is to share. Group members read the same material at the same time and then talk about it. Each member of the circle is equal and participation should be equal among all group members.

Much attention is currently being paid to Literature Circles in the classroom. Many different perspectives, alternatives, and versions are emerging as teachers experiment and encourage students to participate. Having a clear idea of what Literature Circles are helps to establish the direction you wish to take. We see Literature Circles like this.

**A Literature Circle is:**

- a methodology that helps students communicate as readers.

- a forum for students to articulate their thoughts, opinions, predictions, and questions about common material they have read.

- a forum that provides students with opportunities to interact with reading material at different levels. Students examine the literal aspects of the book, make connections to their own lives, and seek out elements of the story they feel are important.

- an activity that helps to establish positive reading behaviors in students by demonstrating cooperation and communication within groups. A Literature Circle invites students to be part of a community of readers. Students take part in discussions with other readers with varied backgrounds and reading experiences. By encountering others' reactions and opinions to literature, students develop a better understanding of their own views and thoughts.

**A Literature Circle is not:**

- a reading program. It is only one aspect of a well-rounded, effective reading program.

- a reading group that focuses on the attainment of decoding skills.

- a novel study, in which the teacher presents a concentrated focus on a book to explore central themes.

- about homogenous groups. One goal of Literature Circles is to promote diversity—in thoughts, skills, perceptions, and views.

- activity based. It is process oriented and provides active learning in the classroom.

- teacher oriented. It is about the classroom being a student-centered place for children to freely and spontaneously discuss and explore literature. The teacher acts as a facilitator.

# The Value of Literature Circles

There are many benefits to using Literature Circles as part of your reading program. Not only do they contribute to improved reading ability in students, but they also help to develop better communication skills and a sense of community in the classroom.

**Communication:** Students enter our classrooms with a series of multiple intelligences and skills. These include the ability to successfully interact with others. Students with an aptitude for communication thrive in Literature Circle sessions, and may have more success with reading than in other literacy activities. For those who lack confidence in their ability to communicate, the small group setting provides a safe environment for sharing.

**Quality of reading:** The quality of reading in which students engage during Literature Circles is often superior to independent reading sessions. Students become eager to share their opinions with their peers, and they feel there is another purpose to their reading other than entertainment. They will therefore focus more on the content, style, and themes of the literature.

**Sense of Community:** Literature Circles help to develop a sense of community. Often, it is hard to find the right method to create a sense of community in readers. While not tangible, a sense of community is critical in long-term goals of reading. Literature Circles assist in the achievement of such goals. Students like the idea of being part of a group and of having the power to express their thoughts, especially if they have never experienced either. Literature Circles invite students to engage in the process on their own, and to seek out others with the same interests.

# LITERATURE CIRCLES MANAGEMENT

Before you start your class with Literature Circles, we recommend you do the following:

**Decide how many students will be in each group.** We recommend five students per group as the optimum number. In Literature Circles, each student has one or two roles to play that help start and maintain discussion. Five per group works well in terms of the number of roles and also allows for absenteeism without compromising discussions. Fewer than five students increase the chances of pairing off, while six or more in a group reduce each student's chance to participate.

**Collect books and stories for your classroom.** There are many different ways you can start to build up a book collection. Book clubs and interlibrary loans work well, but we also scour used bookstores and try to add a few new titles to our collection each year. Collect five copies (one per student) of each book or story that will fit the various levels of your students. We provide six short stories that will help you teach the roles, but you will also need a number of other stories and books to run Literature Circles during the year. We find the following books work well.

## Picture Books

*The Artist* by John Bianchi (1993, Bungalo Books)

*Wild Weather Soup* by Caroline Formby (1995, Child's Play International)

*Hey, Al* by Arthur Yorinks (1987, Farrar)

*The Tenth Good Thing About Barney* by Judith Viorst (1975, Aladdin Paperbacks)

*Ira Sleeps Over* by Bernard Waber (1972, Houghton Mifflin)

*Sleep Out* by Carol and Donald Carrick (1973, Clarion Books)

*Alexander and the Terrible, Horrible, No Good, Very Bad Day* by Judith Viorst (1972, Atheneum)

## Novels

*Missing May* by Cynthia Rylant (1993, Orchard Books)

*Shiloh* by Phyllis Reynolds Naylor (1992, Atheneum)

*Sarah, Plain and Tall* by Patricia McLachlan (1986, HarperCollins)

*The Whipping Boy* by Sid Fleischman (1989, Greenwillow)

*Bridge To Terabithia* by Katherine Patterson (1978, Crowell)

*The 18th Emergency* by Betsy Byars (1973, Viking)

*The Pinballs* by Betsy Byars (1977, Viking)

*Abel's Island* by William Steig (1976, Farrar)

*Charlotte's Web* by E.B. White (1952, HarperCollins)

*A Question of Trust* by Marion Dane Bauer (1994, Apple Paperbacks)

*Search for the Shadowman* by Joan Lowery Nixon (1996, Yearling Books)

*The Castle in the Attic* by Elizabeth Winthrop (1985, Yearling Books)

*Night of the Twisters* by Ivy Ruckman (1984, HarperCollins)

*Poppy* by Avi (1995, Avon Books)

**Work out a schedule.** We found the most manageable time frame for Literature Circles runs for a four- or five-week block. Any shorter period seems rushed, and a longer time period drags the process out. Since all the groups run at the same time, we try to collaborate with students to set up a schedule for discussion periods, work periods, and extension activities.

We have included a sample monthly planner (fig. 1). This planner shows how we allow ample time for role preparation and reading and indicates group meeting times. This kind of chart helps students organize themselves to meet deadlines, and it can also carry through to other parts of the student's curriculum.

**Have all role worksheets ready ahead of time, and copied on different colored paper.** Students can then easily find a page in their notebook; for example, use a green sheet of paper for the Relater's Job and white paper for the Picture Maker.

| Literature Circle Planner for __MAY "BRIDGE TO TERABITHIA__ | | | | |
|---|---|---|---|---|
| **MONDAY** | **TUESDAY** | **WEDNESDAY** | **THURSDAY** | **FRIDAY** |
| 1 READ | 2 FINISH READING P.28 | 3 PREPARE FOR ROLE | 4 MEETING #1 | 5 READ (HAVE TITLE PAGE DONE) |
| 8 FINISH READING p.56 | 9 PREPARE FOR ROLE | 10 MEETING #2 | 11 READ | 12 FINISH READING P.77 |
| 15 PREPAE FOR ROLE | 16 MEETING #3 | 17 READ | 18 FINISH READING P.102 | 19 PREPARE FOR ROLE |
| 22 NO SCHOOL | 23 MEETING #4 | 24 READ | 25 FINISH BOOK | 26 PREPARE FOR ROLE |
| 29 MEETING #5 | 30 WRAP-UP | 31 EXTENSION ACTIVITIES | | |

FIGURE 1. SAMPLE

**Have a storage system.** Students should each have a three-hole binder or folder to use for storing all materials related to Literature Circles.

**Divide the books into five sections;** one per role.

**Use Post-it Notes.** We buy a bulk supply of the small size and distribute a portion to each student at the beginning of the Literature Circle. As students read each section of the book and prepare themselves for their roles, we show them how to use Post-it Notes for taking notes.

## Setting up Literature Circles

When we started using Literature Circles we tried having loosely structured discussions with the students in small and large groups. As with all group work, we found inequities among members in terms of participation, shyness, and leadership. The discussions worked well when we were the guides, but faltered when we were not involved. This indicated that students were not sure of their roles in their groups, which in turn meant that the discussions were not productive. Without specific role assignments, students did not have the confidence to articulate their opinions and ideas about the literature.

We needed to create independence, and we found the best way to do this was to assign roles. We find it is the best method to structure Literature Circles, and our students appreciate knowing what is expected of them each session.

## The Roles

Daniels (1994) provided a framework for assigning roles in Literature Circle groups. With roles to play, students can develop their discussions, create the necessary dialogue, and make the discussions about literature as productive as possible.

We have compiled a list of roles, a strategy for teaching each role and the dynamics of group

communication through mini-lessons, and a number of short stories that teachers can use to help students understand their role in the Literature Circle.

We define the roles as follows:

**The Highlighter:** The Highlighter reads aloud two sections of the story. Each section should be one or two paragraphs in length. The Highlighter chooses whatever he or she feels should be highlighted. It can be a funny section, a sad section, or a confusing section. The Highlighter then asks the others in the group why they think these sections were chosen.

**The Relater:** The Relater finds connections between the story and the world in which he or she lives (their reality). The student should find two or three connections. The others in the group suggest why the Relater chose the sections.

**The Picture Maker:** The Picture Maker uses his or her imagination to interpret part of the story visually. The picture can be a sketch, painting, cartoon, diagram, or collage. It should represent a feeling or idea from the story.

**The Word Detective:** The Word Detective comes to the group with three special words, ready to explain the meaning of each. The words might be unfamiliar to the student, or may simply sound interesting, prompting the Word Detective to study the root and meaning of each.

**The Profiler:** The Profiler chooses one main character and tries to determine what kind of personality the character has, based on the description of appearance, and what he or she says and does. The Profiler lists and explains the personality traits and cites three examples of each trait in the story.

**The Question Maker:** The Question Maker prepares questions that will start the group discussion. The Question Maker learns the difference between open- and closed-ended questions (big and little questions). He/she asks questions to all members of the group, and maintains the flow of conversation within the group.

When the Question Maker role is shared among the group members, have each student come to the group with one question.

We suggest two options for dividing the roles among the group members. (1) Each student has a separate role for which he or she is solely responsible or (2) each student has one role to play, and the role of the Question Maker is shared among the members of the group. The Question Maker is not meant to be the group's leader, but we have found that in option 1, the student in this role often leads and guides the session. In option 2, we can minimize the perception that the Question Maker is the 'leader' in the Literature Circle. Literature Circles are meant to promote shared learning, so having one student perceived as the leader is counterproductive to the process. We prefer option two.

## Teaching the Roles

Before you can begin teaching the roles, you need to do some pre-planning and decision making. Once you decide on the number of students in each group, you must plan how to teach the roles. To help, we have included six short stories in Part 4 of this book for you to photocopy and use.

While there is no specific order in which to teach the roles, we usually hold off on the Question Maker role until students feel comfortable with the process and after the mini-lesson on questioning. We have found that it is best to teach one role per day over the first two weeks. This allows students to understand each role equally.

### Option 1

Since five members is the optimum number for Literature Circles, we use five different roles, one for each student. We remove the Profiler role and substitute it with the Question Maker. With the Question Maker role played by one student, he or she is expected to provide three or four questions for the group.

If you feel the Profiler role needs to be included, you can remove one of the other roles instead. We do recommend that the Question Maker remain one of the roles at all times as it provides the initial stimulus to generate discussion.

- Highlighter
- Relater
- Picture Maker
- Word Detective
- Question Maker

### Option 2

In option 2, the Literature Circle group has five students, each with one role (Picture Maker, Word Detective, Highlighter, Relater, Profiler), but they are each also a Question Maker. Each student must bring questions to the group but have also prepared a separate role. They ask their questions first, and then present their roles. At each session, a different person starts the session. When students share the role of Question Maker it takes longer for them to complete their discussion. It also means the initial teaching requires instruction of six roles, but it creates equality in the groups.

- Highlighter
- Relater
- Picture Maker
- Word Detective
- Profiler
- Question Maker (shared)

Figure 2. Teaching the roles

Figure 3. Playing the arena

Use the handouts from Part 2 to teach the roles in your Literature Circles. Distribute a copy of each role description to each student. Students should add these to their Literature Circles notebook. At the same time, distribute and discuss the working sheets. Before teaching the roles, copy and hand out as many sets of the short stories as you need.

For each role, read the corresponding story aloud. Break the class into groups of five where each member shares his or her understanding of the assigned role. Observe the discussion groups, and look for those students who are at ease with the process and for those who may need future guidance.

After the small groups have finished, the class resumes for a final debriefing to share thoughts, talk about what went well, and discuss any areas that need improvement. Repeat this process for each role over two weeks.

When Literature Circles are in full gear, we divide the role descriptions and work sheets into piles and assign each role a number. The Highlighter job is given number one, Relater is number two, and Picture Maker is number three, for example. Each group member is assigned a number and

starts with the coinciding role. When the Literature Circle starts, each group member starts with his or her assigned number and proceeds to the next. One student may start with role number three, then proceed to four, five, one, and then two.

## Playing the Arena

Playing the arena allows us to make sure the groups function well. This is a demonstration of Literature Circles in action, so the students can learn by example. To make sure all groups will function optimally, we spend some time playing the 'arena'—demonstrating a Literature Circle.

As the roles are taught, observe and then choose students who feel at ease with the process. We call upon four students to do a demonstration of Literature Circles in action. The whole class reads a simple short story to become familiar with the content. The four demonstrators (with the teacher acting as the fifth group member) select a role and are given the assignment to prepare for the next day.

The next day the group meets in front of the class in a Literature Circle. They spend the necessary amount of time discussing the reading, and playing their roles as a demonstration for the rest of the class to observe. We stop the discussion periodically to point out strengths and weaknesses in the process. At the end of the discussion, the participants' performances are discussed and suggestions are made on what they could do differently in the future. This quick two-day demonstration helps cut down on future management difficulties and saves time in the long run.

# Mini-Lessons

As the roles are taught, we follow with a set of mini-lessons on group dynamics, communication, and general instruction on how to make Literature Circles successful. Though the students are concentrating on learning the roles, there are also a number of issues surrounding group work and communication that the students will have to deal with once they start their group work.

Working in groups is not necessarily a natural process for many students, and the skills needed to work successfully with others need to be taught. We have developed a number of mini-lessons that will help students understand how to communicate better, voice their opinions, and work effectively in their groups.

Being a strong reader does not necessarily mean a student will excel in Literature Circles. At the same time, weaker readers can experience unexpected success. How students interact with others in their group will partly determine how well they do. Literature Circles give opportunities to all levels of reader, and all levels of communicator, both experiencing success and building skills.

We have included mini-lesson handouts in Part 2 for students to keep in their Literature Circle notebooks. You may also want to make large posters to put up in the classroom.

## Mini-Lesson #1: Group Work

Starting a Literature Circle discussion is easy; maintaining it is not. We need to offer tips to our students on how to maintain effective discussions. This lesson offers suggestions and cues that students can use in their Literature Circles. While they may not immediately start using the cues, continued modeling and guidance will help them become better conversationalists.

## Mini-Lesson #2: Big Questions & Little Questions

Effective questioning is a skill that is learned. Students need to learn how to use questions to get useful responses, and to maintain flow in discussions. The concept of "big questions" and "little questions" is one way to show students how to create effective questions. Use a story that everyone is familiar with, and practice constructing "big questions" that will elicit longer and more complex answers.

## Mini-Lesson #3: A Personality Profile

In most works of fiction, the character drives the plot. To help students understand character they must be able to connect literature to personality and emotions. Often students understand emotions and personalities, but they do not have the vocabulary to attach them with characters in the stories.

To help students become more familiar with character traits we provide a list of useful descriptors. Review and discuss the personality list with the class, and have the students look up or explore words they do not understand.

FIGURE 4. RESPONSE jouNAliNg

**Mini-Lesson #4: Response Journals**

While group discussions are key to student development, a tangible record of a Literature Circle is sometimes needed. We use a response journal that can take on many forms, depending on its purpose.

Response journals are written records of the students' thoughts, reactions, and perceptions about the story and of the Literature Circles process.

Some teachers have students write a letter to the author, reflecting on their role in the Literature Circle and their reaction to the story. Other teachers have students write a reflection at the end of each session and record it in their workbooks.

You can decide which method best suits your students. Regular reporting sometimes allows students to be more reflective about their reading and reactions to it, while writing something at the end of Literature Circles provides excellent closure for other students.

In Part 2, we have included a sample of a response journal that records reactions to a short story we use to teach the roles. We also have students write an initial response to the idea of Literature Circles as practice journaling.

## Book Talk and Group Formation

After you have prepared, planned, taught roles and communication skills, and collected enough books, you can move your Literature Circles into full gear. The next step to implementing Literature Circles is Book Talk. Book Talk helps students formulate the criteria on which to base their book or story selection. Selecting books is key to how the groups will look in the final Literature Circle, so Book Talk is important to the final dynamics that will play out when the students are in their discussion groups. We prefer to give the students the choice of what they will read, but we help guide their decisions. Seven to eight different titles, with a minimum of five copies of each, should be available for students to look at.

To start Book Talk, students review all the titles. We then talk about each book, read the back cover, show the front cover, and comment on the author(s). After our review, we have the students decide on their top three choices. We remind them about the importance of making choices based on reading ability and interest in the topic (as opposed to choosing what their friends choose). We often use ballots that include the student's name and choices. This helps to avoid peer pressure in the selection process. Emphasize that it is important to carefully consider all three choices. Due to logistics we cannot guarantee their first choice, but we try our best to assign students to at least one of their options.

We remind students that part of being in a Literature Circle is hearing new views. When we create the groups, we take into account all kinds of dynamics such as pairing less verbal students with more verbal ones. We try to balance the groups with both girls and boys, and we do our best to mix weaker and stronger readers in the same group. As the year progresses and students become more comfortable working together, and understand the Literature Circle process and benefits, we start to let them make their own groups.

Once the students have selected their story or book, and the groups are formed, you can move the class into a planning session in preparation for the Literature Circle.

## The Group Planning Session

In the first meeting, we give each student his/her story and a blank calendar, and we work together to schedule the Literature Circle sessions (fig. 6). In each group, the students divide their novel into five sections, looking for reasonable gaps and stopping points on certain pages. The group members come to a consensus on scheduling the reading sessions, preparation sessions, and meeting sessions. Response journaling should also be scheduled throughout the term. We have found that Literature Circles work best when they are held every third day. While the calendar is filled out, we also pass out the role work sheet handouts for students to add to their Literature Circle binder.

This is a good time to establish the essential rules of conduct for Literature Circle meetings. You probably have rules for classroom conduct that you establish at the beginning of the school year, but group work has specific challenges for students who are new to the process. We make the process of establishing rules of conduct a class activity and include the students' feedback in establishing guidelines. We start with a brainstorming session where we ask, "What does it take for a group to succeed while working together on a project?" Students come up with good ideas for proper group conduct, though we find that they often have trouble articulating them clearly. We guide them in clarifying what they mean, and we record what they say on flip charts. The end result is a list of ideas on how to succeed as a group. It is a good idea to post the

Figure 5. Group planning session

ideas somewhere in the classroom where students are reminded of what they came up with. Have a student enter the list in the computer, and pass that out to students as well. In Part 2, we have included a list of guidelines that you can copy and give to your students. We go through the list with the class to emphasize how group dynamics should work in Literature Circles. Combined with the mini-lessons, students have a very good idea of how to act respectfully and cooperatively in their groups. Spending time explaining group behavior before your students start working in their groups will likely avoid problems in communication once they form their Literature Circles.

Once students are comfortable with the idea of working together they will begin assigning tasks and role preparation as homework. To begin, however, we prefer to use class time for meeting and working in groups. Once the groups have met and worked together they will understand the expectations of the group members and

| Literature Circle Planner for _____ | | | | |
|---|---|---|---|---|
| MONDAY | TUESDAY | WEDNESDAY | THURSDAY | FRIDAY |
| | | | | |
| | | | | |
| | | | | |
| | | | | |
| | | | | |

Figure 6. Sample weekly/monthly planner

the teacher. They become aware of what happens if they do not prepare, and of how their work affects the success of every member of the group. An unprepared group in Literature Circles is a disaster!

The sample yealy plan (fig. 7) shows how to divide the year into workable Literature Circle segments. As the year progresses, less time is needed to prepare roles. You can schedule more Literature Circles in the winter as a result.

| A Sample Yearly Plan | |
|---|---|
| Mid-September | ○ Teach the roles using short stories (two-week period) <br> ○ Teach mini-lessons on group dynamics, roles, etc. |
| October | ○ Playing the arena <br> ○ Book talk <br> ○ Divide students into groups |
| November | ○ Students work through books and hold group discussions <br> ○ Prepare for extension activities |
| December | ○ Students work on extension activities (2 weeks) <br> ○ Students present extension activities |
| Late January/February | ○ Second series of Literature Circles takes place (four-week period + two weeks for extension activities) |
| April-May | ○ A final third round of Literature Circles (4–6 weeks) <br> ○ Literature Circles adaptations, Poetry Circles, Math Circles, etc. |

Figure 7. Sample

# EXTENSION ACTIVITIES

What happens after the students finish reading, discussing, and evaluating the book or story? We have found that they often want more! They need a sense of closure after having invested so many hours in the book or story. We think extension activities are a good way to end the Literature Circle. It is a tangible method of assessment, and it allows the students to summarize what they have read and discussed. Extension activities for Literature Circles give students a chance to use another voice in their discussions. You provide options, guidance, and some structure to these projects. The students select projects as a group.

To ensure the project is not the sole purpose of the grades-driven student, we explain to our classes that these projects are a way of sharing the books we have read. Whatever project the students choose, they should understand that they will share it with the whole class, not just hand in something to the teacher. Students begin to understand how literature can be connected to other forms of creative communication such as art, drama, music, or theater. They understand that they are trying to bring the story to life for the rest of the class.

You provide background and resources about the different creative media from which the students can choose. The extension activity is creative outlet for the students, and allows interdisciplinary activities to open up different and valuable ways of looking at the same thing. Perhaps a student will choose to interpret the written story with poetry or with watercolors. He/she might decide to sing a song or write a play. You can guide all these activities, but try to encourage maximum creativity on the student's part. At the same time, you may have to set guidelines for the activity so students do not get too carried away. Expectations and goals can be clarified early, as students organize their projects. We like to set a guideline of two weeks maximum for completion of the extension activity.

Part of the assessment of the extension project is in the group process itself. Within groups, there are often both leaders and those who do not contribute as much. Watching the dynamics within the working groups is part of the teacher's job. Often we try to guide the students on how to more efficiently spend their valuable time. We usually suggest that the group assign each member a task he or she can work on individually and be able to bring back to the group as part of the overall project.

Over two weeks of extension activities, we schedule class time for working on the extension projects. Students are also expected to work outside of class time. As the two-week time period draws to a close, we set up a schedule for presentations.

Figure 8. Extension Projects

Each group presents the book and extension project to the rest of the class. The class is invited to comment and ask questions. We find extension project presentations help build a sense of community among our readers. These presentations also create interest in the books that other students may not have read.

Following are some successful extension projects our students have enjoyed.

## Extension Projects

### Character Box

A character box is like a mini-museum. It contains artifacts (objects), or models of artifacts, that are important to the characters in the book. The objects are put on display with information cards explaining how they relate to the book. Most artifacts are miniatures of the objects that would be found in the story. An example may be a Little Red Riding Hood Character box. Inside, you may find a small hand-made picnic basket, representing the one carried by Little Red Riding Hood; or a piece of red cloth from her cloak. A miniature axe belonging to the woodcutter or a picture of wolves would also be appropriate.

### New Ending

Sometimes stories do not end the way you had hoped. This extension activity gives the students a chance to change the ending. The group rewrites the ending to reflect the discussions they had in their Literature Circle. They might decide to add something, re-explain, or re-invent something about the ending.

It is important that the group not reveal the real ending to the story. Presenting the alternate ending should create some curiosity for the other students to read the story themselves. This contributes to the community of readers in the class.

### Picture Collage

"A picture is worth a thousand words." A collage is a collection of pictures that represents the words and ideas students have read in their stories. Students cut out pictures, words, or images, and mount them on a poster board. The images they choose represent discussions they have had about the story.

### Game/Puzzle Book

Students can develop a game or puzzle book. The book can be a word search, a crossword puzzle, match-up puzzle, fill-in-the-blank game, or a quiz game that uses words from the story. When other students work on the game book they will have to go through the story to find the answers.

### Play

Theater can be an excellent medium to represent the story or book. The group produces a short play based on the story they have read. The group re-writes the dialogue and performs in front of the class. Students may have to create costumes and sets or find appropriate props for the play, but it is a good way to incorporate a number of different art forms.

## Mini Research Sheets

This activity combines entertainment with facts found in the story. Information in the story may have triggered curiosity in the students, leading to further interest in researching it. Students find more information about certain issues, and create a reference sheet of facts that others might find interesting.

If the group reads a story about a boy and his dog, they might decide to look for more information about dogs. The benefit and fun in this activity comes when students dig deeply for interesting information about a subject—'a dog has four legs' or 'a dog barks' is not acceptable.

Once the information is collected, students can compile it in a poster presentation. A "Did You Know?" poster should mention what inspired the group to do research in this area, and each member of the group should be well versed in the information so all questions from the class can be answered.

## More Extension Projects

Here are more ideas for projects that work well for extension activities.

- advertisement posters
- a reader's theatre
- a time line of the story
- a newspaper article
- an interview with one of the characters
- a profile of the author
- a mobile with illustrations and facts
- a new cover for the story
- a diorama of a scene
- an excerpt from a diary of one character
- an alphabet book based on the story
- song lyrics/CD insert for the story
- poems on the book
- a puppet show based on the story
- a coat of arms for a character
- a flag to represent the story
- a video box case/video advertisements for the story
- a painting/sculpture
- postcards from the characters
- a board game
- a number book based on the story
- an advice column for the characters
- a home designed for the main character
- a comic strip based on the book
- other similar books grouped together for a presentation
- a map for your story
- bookmarks with illustrations and facts on them
- a dictionary based on the story
- page of quotations (select important phrases and dialog)
- a list of top ten reasons for reading the story
- a book review

# Evaluating Students in Their Literature Circles

Literature Circles are student based and process oriented. The evaluation process involves student self-assessment and reflection; however, the teacher still requires a method of assessment to ensure students are benefiting from the program.

We have arranged our assessment process in three stages where we evaluate:

- the preparation and planning stage
- the discussion stage
- the follow-up stage

## Assessing Preparation and Planning

Assessing preparation is best achieved through observation and with students during preparation time. Circulate throughout the groups, recording notes on each student.

- Assess how prepared the students are in their Literature Circle.
- Look for organization of material, e.g., keeping up with assigned reading, and having roles well prepared to exhibit reading comprehension.

## Assessing Discussion

Circulate throughout discussion groups, recording observations.

- Look for the quality of discussion.

- Reflect on how discussion affects the way each student thinks about the text.

## Student Responses and Follow-Up

There are three parts to the follow-up stage that you can assess

1.  Response Journals: read and evaluate the journals after every session

2.  Extension projects: assess the project after it has been completed

3.  Oral Presentations: assess the presentation

In response journals, students demonstrate their understanding of literature, and they show that they are reflecting on their own reactions to what they are reading.

Assessing the extension projects requires that you evaluate the connections to the story and the completeness of the students interpretations.

Assessment of the verbal presentation of the extension project is centered on presentation skills such as using the proper voice and making eye contact with the audience.

## Using Rubrics

Since so much of the evaluation process is based on observation and anecdotal comments, the use of rubrics can help lend structure. We have designed rubrics to help you assess the students. Part 3 of this book contains a number of rubrics for assessing all areas of Literature Circles.

PART 2

# HANDOUTS

# Getting Involved

Literature Circles can be fun. It is exciting to be part of a group that shares something. So get involved, read, think, and talk about books!

## Responsibilities of a Member

Remember—a Literature Circle is a team, and you are part of that team. Each team member has responsibilities that are defined by the role he or she is assigned.

## People Are Depending On You

When you are assigned a role, others in the group are counting on you to bring the necessary work to the next meeting. It is important that you keep up with the reading, and always have your copy of the story with you. It is hard to be a valued member of the team if you do not know what is going on. Remember—people want to hear from you and talk to you about the story.

## Participation Is Important

Some people enjoy talking and sharing their ideas, while others prefer to be quiet. Since all members are expected to participate equally, you need to ask yourself: Do I need to speak up more? Do I need to hold back and listen more?

## Think It Through

You will be presenting and hearing some original and well-thought-out ideas about the story you read. Literature Circles will give you great learning opportunities. As you read your assigned pages, take the time to think through what you are reading. The more prepared you are, the more ideas you will be able to discuss in the group.

# Literature Circles Guidelines

Here are some guidelines for you to follow so your group works together in a friendly and fun way.

1. **Cooperate.** Not everyone will have the same opinion. That is okay, but you still need to get along with one another. Be aware of others' feelings, be polite, and respect each member of the group.

2. **Agree to disagree.** At times, you will have to put your own views aside and accept an opinion or decision with which you may not agree.

3. **Be considerate of each other.** Treat people the way you want to be treated.

4. **Help each other.** Remember that you are a team. Everybody has different strengths and weaknesses. If you see someone struggling, offer to help. You never know when you might need assistance in return.

5. **One person talks at a time.** Everybody's opinion is valuable and deserves to be heard. If everybody is talking at once, some important views may not be heard.

6. **Use a proper speaking voice.** You are in a group, and people want to hear from you. Speak in a voice that can be heard and is easy to listen to. Look at people when you are speaking to them. Do not talk too quietly or too loudly. Use an appropriate speaking voice.

7. **Listen to one another.** Do not concentrate just on what you want to say. Listen to what others have to say. Someone might say something to change your mind about what you were planning to talk about.

8. **Disagree but...** Everybody has opinions. When your opinion differs from someone else's it is okay to express disagreement. Arguing, however, can leave people with hurt feelings. Talk calmly, and accept that some people will go along with what you say and some will have their own views.

9. **Stay on topic.** You are in your Literature Circle to share your views on the reading. Try and stay on this topic. If you have other matters to talk about with members of the group, save those discussions for another time.

# Role: The Highlighter

Choose two passages from the story to read aloud. Each passage should be two paragraphs long. It can be funny, sad, confusing, or important to the story in some other way.

Once you have chosen a passage, record the information on your work sheet. Remember to give a reason or justification for your selection.

When it is your turn to present, tell the others in your group what page and paragraph to turn to. Read your selection to the group.

Ask each member of the group why he or she thinks you chose the passage you did. Listen to their comments, then tell them why you chose the section to highlight.

# HIGHLIGHTER WORK SHEET

**Highlighted Section 1:** Page:_____ Paragraph: _____

Reminder:  Reasons for highlighting
- ○  an enjoyable part
- ○  a funny part
- ○  a scary part
- ○  an interesting part
- ○  a good description
- ○  a major event
- ○  a well-written part
- ○  many other reasons

Why I picked it.  (Explain in paragraph form.)  _____

_____

_____

_____

_____

_____

**Highlighted Section 2:** Page:_____ Paragraph: _____

Reminder:  Reasons for highlighting
- ○  an enjoyable part
- ○  a funny part
- ○  a scary part
- ○  an interesting part
- ○  a good description
- ○  a major event
- ○  a well-written part
- ○  many other reasons

Why I picked it.  (Explain in paragraph form.)  _____

_____

_____

_____

_____

# Role: The Relater

As the Relater, it is your job to find connections between the story and your world. Stories remind us about other things— when you connect a story you have just read to other ideas, you are **relating ideas.**

Choose a section that reminds you of something from your own life or from the life of someone you know. On the work sheet, explain how your experience is similar to the one you selected in the book. Find two to three relationships between you and the book.

In your group, explain the real-life experience you can connect to the story. Ask others in your group to figure out where in the story there is a similar situation. After everyone has had a chance to make a prediction, reveal the page and scene in the story where the relationship can be found. Explain how your experience and the situation in the book are similar.

# R E L A T E R   W O R K   S H E E T

Some relationships I found between this reading and my own life or the life of someone I know.

**Relationship 1:** Page:_____ Paragraph: _____

Real-Life Relationship/Relationship to Others (books, movies, TV, songs, etc.) _____

_____

_____

_____

_____

_____

_____

_____

**Relationship 2:** Page:_____ Paragraph: _____

Real-Life Relationship/Relationship to Others (books, movies, TV, songs, etc.) _____

_____

_____

_____

_____

_____

_____

_____

# Role: The Picture Maker

You will use the story to create a picture, sketch, cartoon, diagram, chart, or collage. You can re-create a picture from the book, or create an image of something that the reading reminds you of. Your picture can represent a feeling or an idea.

Without saying anything, show your picture to the others in your group. Ask them if they can identify the scene from the story.

After everyone has had a chance to comment on your illustration, explain what the picture means and what part of the story it depicts.

# PICTURE MAKER WORK SHEET

On the reverse side of this work sheet, complete your illustration, diagram, chart, cartoon, collage, etc.

This picture is about...

_____

_____

_____

_____

_____

_____

_____

_____

I decided to do this picture because...

_____

_____

_____

_____

_____

_____

_____

_____

# Role: The Word Detective

○

Your job is to choose three special words from the story. These words might be unfamiliar to you, they might sound interesting, or they may seem important to you for another reason.

On your Word Detective work sheet, write down the page number and section where each word is found. Look up the meanings of the words in a dictionary, and record the definitions on your work sheet. For words with more than one meaning, select the one that best fits with how the word is used in the story.

Tell the others which page contains the first word, and read the definition, but not the word. Ask the others in your group to find the word that you are talking about. Once the word has been identified, explain your reason for selecting it.

# WORD DETECTIVE WORK SHEET

Word: _____ Page: _____ Paragraph: _____

Definition: _____

_____

_____

_____

_____

_____

_____

Word: _____ Page: _____ Paragraph: _____

Definition: _____

_____

_____

_____

_____

_____

_____

Word: _____ Page: _____ Paragraph: _____

Definition: _____

_____

_____

_____

_____

_____

_____

# Role: The Profiler

Your job is to look at the characters and determine their personalities based on how they act, what they say, and how you imagine they look.

On your Profiler work sheet, record a personality trait for one of the characters. Find three examples in the story where the character exhibits that trait. Alternately, you might identify three different personality traits for one character, and show evidence for each trait. In your group, read your three examples from the story and let the other group members try to identify the personality trait(s).

# PROFILER WORK SHEET

Character:_____

Personality Trait: _____, _____, _____

**Evidence 1:**  Page: _____  Paragraph: _____

Description of action, appearance, speech, thoughts. _____

_____

_____

_____

_____

**Evidence 2:**  Page: _____  Paragraph: _____

Description of action, appearance, speech, thoughts. _____

_____

_____

_____

_____

**Evidence 3:**  Page: _____  Paragraph: _____

Description of action, appearance, speech, thoughts. _____

_____

_____

_____

_____

# Role: The Question Maker

Your job is to prepare questions that will start the group discussion and allow the members to share their opinions. After you have read the story very carefully, record your questions on your Question Maker work sheet.

Try to avoid asking closed-ended questions (those that can be answered with a one word answer like 'yes' or 'no'). Be sure to pose a question to each member of the group so that everyone has an equal chance to participate.

# QUESTION MAKER WORK SHEET

**Possible Discussion Questions**

Question 1: _____

_____

_____

_____

Question 2: _____

_____

_____

_____

Question 3: _____

_____

_____

_____

Question 4: _____

_____

_____

_____

Question 5: _____

_____

_____

_____

# Mini-Lesson #1:
# Group Work

## Keeping discussion alive

Creating and maintaining good discussion requires a lot of hard work. In a discussion one person might be able to start, but it takes the participation of the whole group to keep it alive. How can you keep the discussion from faltering?

- Share your comments. Don't be shy!

- Respond to what other members say.

- Add in a question. Ask someone to further explain something, ask the group members what they think about something or what makes them think that way.

- Add or expand on what someone else has said.

Here are some conversation starters that will help your discussion stay on track.

- That reminds me...

- I thought the same way except...

- What makes you think that...

- I'm glad you said that because...

- So, what do you think about...

- I was wondering if anyone else noticed...

- Could anyone help me figure out...

- I am curious to know...

- I thought a little differently...

Can you think of anything else that would help to keep a conversation going? _____

_____

_____

_____

_____

_____

_____

# Mini-Lesson #2: Big Questions &
## Little Questions

Some questions have short answers (like 'yes' or 'no'). These are called little questions. Some questions require longer, more in-depth answers. These are called big questions.

Little questions require simple answers. Ask yourself the following questions, and notice how short your answers are:

How old are you?

Which character is the thief?

Where did the story take place?

Which character do you like?

Do you like the setting of the story?

How many pets does the character have?

Do you think the character did the right thing?

Big questions are better for discussion because the answers require more thought and often lead to more questions. To make your Literature Circle more fun and more interesting, try to ask big questions. Some examples are:

Why do you like that character?

In what way would you change the setting of the story?

Why do you think the character has so many pets?

If you were the character how would you handle things?

What did the character do next?

Why did the character act the way he/she did?

# Mini-Lesson #3:
# A Personality Profile

## 101 Ways To Be

People have many different feelings, called *emotions*. People experience all kinds of emotions at different times, depending on what is happening to them or on what is going on around them.

Personality consists of emotions that are with you most of the time. For example, some people find things funny almost all the time. It is not just a feeling but part of their personality. We say they "have a good sense of humor."

Go through the list of emotions and personalities. Think of times when you experienced each of them.

| | | | |
|---|---|---|---|
| aloof | deceitful | happy | pleased |
| angry | dejected | heartless | polite |
| argumentative | demanding | honest | proud |
| bashful | depressed | humble | reckless |
| blue | devastated | humorous | resentful |
| boastful | dishonest | impatient | resourceful |
| bored | disorganized | indecisive | responsible |
| bossy | distracted | insecure | restless |
| brave | ecstatic | intelligent | revengeful |
| calm | embarrassed | interested | rude |
| carefree | energetic | irresponsible | sarcastic |
| caring | envious | jealous | secretive |
| cautious | excited | kind | self-centered |
| charming | exuberant | lazy | selfish |
| cheerful | fascinated | lonely | shy |
| clever | fearful | loving | silly |
| clumsy | frustrated | meek | sly |
| compassionate | fulfilled | nervous | sorrowful |
| conceited | fun loving | obedient | stubborn |
| confident | fussy | obsessed | suspicious |
| confused | generous | optimistic | sympathetic |
| considerate | giddy | outgoing | thankful |
| content | glad | patient | thoughtful |
| creative | glum | peaceful | vain |
| curious | greedy | pessimistic | witty |
| | | | worried |

# Mini-Lesson #4:
# Response Journal

## Example of a response journal

In a response journal you can write your thoughts, reactions, and perceptions about the story or book you have just read. Here is an example of a letter from one student to the author of a story called *The Feed Me Fire*.

Dear Mr. Rogers:

    I have just finished reading *The Feed Me Fire* and I thought it was great! It was a little spooky but not too scary in a violent kind of way. I could just imagine the two girls feeding the fire non-stop and getting tired.

    When we got into our Literature Circle I was really lucky because I got the job of Picture Maker. I really wanted that job because I already had a picture in my mind that I wanted to illustrate. I drew the part where Morgan tripped with the pot of soup and it landed on the fire. I picked that part because it is very important. It is the solution to the problem.

    We also had to come to our group with some questions. I had no problem coming up with questions. One question I asked the group was do you think the feed me fire was real or was it a dream? I asked everybody and some people said it was a dream because it wasn't realistic. I said I thought it wasn't a dream, and that it didn't have to be realistic if it was a fantasy story. Besides if it was only a dream, where did the soup go in the end?

    That was the other question I asked everybody. What did Dad think about the soup being gone? Do you think he thought somebody ate it? or spilled it out? He would have been in for a big surprise if he found out how it was really used.

    I think I am going to read the story again about five more times. That way I will remember very well. I want to remember it very well so that when my family goes camping this summer I can tell them the story of *The Feed Me Fire*.

Your devoted reader,

Dear Parents and/or Guardians:

During the school year, students will be participating in Literature Circles as part of their reading program. These are discussion-based reading groups, similar to book clubs. In Literature Circles, students choose from a selection of books/ stories, and they are placed in groups along with others who have chosen the same story or book to read. In preparation for their Literature Circle meeting, students read specific sections of the book/story. According to a schedule that they develop as a group, students are also expected to prepare for their role in the meeting. Each student has role expectations on sheets kept in a Literature Circles binder. The purpose for designating roles is to be sure that the discussions run smoothly and are as productive as possible. Students meet every three days to reflect on the reading and share their ideas with others in their group.

At the beginning of the school year, we will go through a series of mini-lessons on how to act in a group situation and on how to best perform the roles. The mini-lessons will show students how to behave, listen, and speak in small groups. You can assist your child by looking through the role handouts, and by becoming familiar with the group's schedule, expectations, and your child's upcoming role. Reading with your child and sharing ideas will help to prepare him/her for the role and will help give him/her the confidence to speak up in the group meetings.

At the end of each Literature Circles session (each lasts from 3-6 weeks), the students complete extension projects about the story/book. There are a number of different projects that they enjoy—poster presentations, plays, puppet shows, songs, inventing word games, and much more. Your child may need help with the project as well.

I look forward to a year of successful Literature Circles, and I hope that you will enjoy spending the time reading with your child! If you have any questions or concerns, please feel free to contact me.

Sincerely,

PART 3

# Rubrics

# Assessment Tools

In the classroom, so much of the evaluation process is based on observation and anecdotal comments. When students are involved in Literature Circles, the use of rubrics can help lend structure to the activity. The following rubrics have been designed to assess the three stages of the Literature Circle process—preperation and planning, discussion, and extension projects. Student self-assessment sheets are also included and can be used in the process of evaluating Literature Circles.

# Preparation and Planning Rubric

1. Student has not completed reading or has not prepared role. Notebook is missing sheets.

2. Student has completed reading and has prepared role. Notebook has all sheets. Role shows evidence of thought.

3. Reading is complete. Role is prepared, and notebook is organized. Role is well developed, showing evidence of analysis of text. Student uses Post-it Notes to highlight sections.

## Preparation of Roles

Literature Circle Time Period (dates):_____

Student Name: _____

Session # _____ Role: _____

Assessment:     1          2          3

Comment: _____

_____

_____

Session # _____ Role: _____

Assessment:     1          2          3

Comment: _____

_____

_____

Session # _____ Role: _____

Assessment:     1          2          3

Comment: _____

_____

_____

# Role Rubrics

## Discussion Sessions

**Highlighter:**

1. Lacks reasoning for selection. Little relevance to themes and issues of the text.

2. Able to provide rationale for choice, and explain how it is related to text. Has some relevance to themes and issues of the text.

3. Selection reflects insight into material. Choice supports central ideas and themes of text.

**Profiler:**

1. Actions or speech of character are misinterpreted.

2. Able to identify specific actions or speech and uses appropriate vocabulary. Selection reflects the character's identity.

3. Able to connect actions and speech to the character's personality.

**Picture Maker:**

1. Image is from an isolated event in the text that is not crucial to the story. Image is messy and lacks clarity.

2. Image represents event from the text that is somewhat pertinent. Image is clear, uses art medium well.

3. Image reflects an important aspect of the story. Exceptional use of art medium, and the images are well developed.

## Relater:

1. Unable to make connection from story to real-life experiences.
2. Connections are mostly concrete, relating events from the text to personal life.
3. Connections show depth and understanding of the text. Relates experiences to text well.

## Question Maker:

1. Questions ask for facts; can be answered in short reply. Mostly closed-ended questions.
2. Questions seek some opinion. Sometimes ask for explanations from fellow students.
3. Questions generate discussion on topic, seek opinion, and provoke new thought or debate. Uses open-ended questions.

## Word Detective:

1. Vocabulary selected is not crucial to the story; previous knowledge of words may exist. Student presents an inaccurate definition.
2. Selects relevant words that may be new or unfamiliar. Student is able to provide an accurate definition of the word.
3. Vocabulary is selected for its importance and use within the text. May be a new word unfamiliar to other students. Proper definition is provided.

# ROLE ASSESSMENT RECORDING SHEET

## Role Assessment

Student Name: _____

Date: _____


Role: _____

Assessment:    1        2        3

Comment: _____


Role: _____

Assessment:    1        2        3

Comment: _____


Role: _____

Assessment:    1        2        3

Comment: _____


Role: _____

Assessment:    1        2        3

Comment: _____


Role: _____

Assessment:    1        2        3

Comment: _____

# Discussion Group Rubric*

1. Uses inappropriate voice for group discussion. Speaks only when addressed or when presenting a role. Does not offer views freely. Responds in short phrases or one-word answers. Attention is not always focused on the group. Does not appear to be listening.

2. Voice is audible and clear for audience size. Shows active participation by volunteering insights to discussion. Speaks in complete thoughts and phrases. Looks at others and addresses the entire group. Appears to be listening

3. Uses expression in voice to elicit answers. Uses prompts to engage all group members into discussion. Makes good use of eye contact. Expresses ideas in a clear fashion with complete thoughts. Builds on others' ideas. Listens well (actively).

*Use in conjunction with roles rubric.

# DISCUSSIONS RECORDING SHEET

Literature Circle Session (dates): _____

Student Name: _____

Discussion #: _____

Assessment:     1          2          3

Comment: _____

Discussion #: _____

Assessment:     1          2          3

Comment: _____

Discussion #: _____

Assessment:     1          2          3

Comment: _____

Discussion #: _____

Assessment:     1          2          3

Comment: _____

Discussion #: _____

Assessment:     1          2          3

Comment: _____

# Extension Projects Rubric

1. Project is incomplete within the time frame. Project does not reflect the themes of the book. Project misses relevant information. Project is disorganized and messy.

2. Project is completed within the time frame. Original thought is used to complete the project. Makes good use of story in the project. Is able to explain rationale for choosing extension project.

3. Extends the ideas of the story in the project. Is able to go beyond the print to create project. Highlights ideas that reflect the central theme to text. Displays creativity and originality in the project. Has a specific reason for choosing the project.

# EXTENSION PROJECT RECORDING SHEET

Students' Names: _____

_____

_____


Type of Extension Project: _____

Completion Date: _____

Group Assessment:      1           2           3

Comments: _____

_____

_____

_____

_____

_____

_____

_____

_____

_____

_____

_____

_____

# Presentation of Project Rubric

1. Student uses inappropriate voice for presentation. Does not make eye contact. Student is unfamiliar with material and reads from notes.

2. Student uses clear and audible voice. Attempts to make eye contact with the audience. Uses proper stance, and displays material well. Knows material well enough to avoid reading, and refers to it easily.

3. Uses an expressive voice to highlight points. Makes eye contact and physical gestures—pointing out material on project. Is able to speak easily about the project without referring to notes.

# EXTENSION PROJECT PRESENTATION
# RECORDING SHEET

Students' Names: _____

_____

_____


Type of Extension Project: _____

Completion Date: _____

Group Assessment:    1        2        3

Comments: _____

_____

_____

_____

_____

_____

_____

_____

_____

_____

_____

_____

_____

_____

# LITERATURE CIRCLE
# PROGRAM EVALUATION

Student Name: _____

Time Period: _____

## Preparation and Planning:

Overall Mark: _____ (see attached assessment sheets)

## Discussion:

Overall Mark: _____ (see attached assessment sheets)

Comments: _____

_____

_____

## Extension Project:

Overall Mark: _____ (see attached assessment sheets)

Comments: _____

_____

_____

## Presentation of Extension Project:

Overall Mark: _____ (see attached assessment sheets)

Comments: _____

_____

_____

_____

# STUDENT SELF-ASSESSMENT

Name: _____

Date of Discussion: _____

**How I would rate myself:**

| **1** | **2** | **3** |
|---|---|---|
| I need to make some improvements | I performed satisfactorily | I did well |

| | | | |
|---|---|---|---|
| I came to the circle well prepared. | 1 | 2 | 3 |
| I participated often. | 1 | 2 | 3 |
| I spoke in a clear voice that was easy to understand. | 1 | 2 | 3 |
| I cooperated with other members. | 1 | 2 | 3 |
| I offered the group good ideas and opinions. | 1 | 2 | 3 |
| I asked thoughtful questions. | 1 | 2 | 3 |
| I listened to others' ideas. | 1 | 2 | 3 |

My goals for the next Literature Circle meeting are: _____

_____

_____

_____

_____

_____

# RESPONSE JOURNALS EVALUATION

Student Name: _____

| | Points | My Evaluation | Teacher Evaluation | Comments |
|---|---|---|---|---|
| Evidence of thinking by the book | 1 2 3 | | | |
| Length | 1 2 3 | | | |
| Mechanics (punctuation, spelling, etc.) | 1 2 3 | | | |
| Organization | 1 2 3 | | | |

# OUR GROUP SESSION ASSESSMENT

Student Name: _____

Date of Meeting: _____

| What We Did Well | What We Need to Improve |
|---|---|
| | |

PART 4

# SHORT STORIES

# Using the Stories to Teach the Roles

We created the following short stories to help explain the roles in Literature Circles. We provide a brief description of each story and suggest which can be used for teaching particular roles.

**The Toad and The Farmer** – We use this story to teach the role of the Highlighter. Its humorous nature always has students eager to read aloud. The story also works well for teaching the Picture Maker and Profiler. Students can debate the nature of the farmer's personality.

**Jack Daw and Joe Crow** – The personality of Mr. Grundy, and the changes we see by the end of the story, illustrate the role of Profiler. Mr. Grundy is described in detail, and he has many personality quirks that are easy for students to pick up on. The story can also be used to teach the role of the Relater. Many of us at some point in our lives have come across a Mr. Grundy or have experienced an event that has changed our views about someone else.

**Plankton** – Students can often relate to Plankton's dilemma. The main character becomes lazy and faces the consequences of his lack of responsibility. This story works well for teaching the role of the Relater, but it can also be used to teach the role of the Question Maker.

**The Feed Me Fire** – This story is descriptive, and students find it fun to illustrate. It is best used for teaching the role of Picture Maker, but also works for teaching the Question Maker and Relater.

**I Remember When** – This story can be used to teach the role of the Word Detective or Relater. By keeping the identity of the characters hidden until the end, the students debate how they interpreted who was speaking and when. Students can reflect on their real-life experiences with family and talking to grandparents. There are good words that the Word Detective can define for the group.

**Rainy and the Lucky Cat Food** – This story helps teach the role of the Picture Maker or Highlighter. Students look for the Fairy Cat Mother's mixed-up dialogue and for anachronisms from the traditional fairy tale. The Relater might find connections to his/her own neighborhood or relationships with adults in this story.

# The Toad and the Farmer

# The Toad and the Farmer

## by Warren Rogers

Farmers can have a lot of problems. Equipment breaks down, insects eat the crops, fields flood, and animals get sick. There once was a farmer who had experienced all these things, but he had an even bigger problem. His wife liked their horse much more than she liked him.

"I can't stand it! You think so much more of that horse of yours than you do of me! Why?" cried the farmer.

"Well, for one thing, my horse doesn't moan and groan and whine about everything the way you do," sneered his wife. "And for another thing, he's cleaner than you."

"That's not fair. Of course I'm dirtier than the horse. I work in the fields all day. The only time that horse has to work is when you take him to town for a ride."

"He's a good companion for me," sniffed the farmer's wife. "Stop feeling sorry for yourself. Don't be so selfish."

"I have to make my own meals. You make FEASTS for that horse of yours, but I'm lucky to get a snack. Yesterday, I had porridge for supper, and the horse got baked carrots and sweet potatoes with oat cakes for dessert! It's just not right. Everyone's laughing at me. You treat me like a stable animal and that...that...horse like a husband!"

"Oh, stop exaggerating. It is not as bad as all that," said his wife. But it was as bad as all that. It was even worse. His wife mended and made special hats and blankets for her horse, but she would not even wash the farmer's clothes, never mind mend or patch them.

One day, the farmer was mumbling and complaining to himself while he was removing stones from the fields. "That horse of hers should be helping to pull out the stones and the stumps. Instead, he gets to graze and laze in a meadow or sleep in his stable. This is most unjust. I have a terrible life."

With a huge grunt and a heave, he turned over a particularly heavy stone.

"Hey, watch it, farm boy!" said a throaty voice. It was a large lumpy toad. "That's my home you just flipped over. What do you think you're doing?"

"Doing?" said the farmer. "I'm doing what I've always done. How is it that you can talk?"

"I can talk because I happen to be a magic field toad. And listen, I'll grant you a wish if you'll put my house back the way it was. Thank you very much."

"Hey, don't I get the usual three wishes?"

"Nope. Sorry. One wish. That's it. Take it or leave it."

"Oh, all right, but it doesn't seem fair. In all the stories, there's always three wishes."

"Phew!" whistled the toad. "Maybe you should wish to stop being such a whiner."

"Great," thought the farmer, "as if it isn't bad enough that my wife insults me. Now I have to hear it from a toad, of all things!" He felt like dropping the big rock on the toad, but he realized one wish was better than no wishes. "Okay, I'll take it."

"I thought you might. Well, put my stone house back the way it was and we have a deal then," ordered the toad.

"I'm going to need some time to think about my one wish," said the farmer as he replaced the stone.

When the farmer returned home, he noticed a really nice hat hanging on the hook on the wall. "Wow, that's a great hat! Do we have company?"

"No, we don't," said his wife. "I bought it as a gift."

"A gift? You mean, you bought it for me? I can't believe it. This is the nicest thing you've done for me since... I can't remember when."

"Who says I bought it for you? I didn't buy it for you, you fool. I bought it for the horse."

"Ahhhh! I can't take this anymore. What about me, your husband? Don't you ever care about me?"

"Oh, don't be silly. You know how to take care of yourself. You're a grown man, for heaven's sake!" And with that she walked out to the barn to put the new hat on her darling horse's head.

"You're going to waste that fine hat on a horse? I can't believe it!" The disgusted farmer walked away muttering, "I wish I had what's on the horse's head."

No sooner had he said these words than he heard his wife screaming. She ran out of the barn with her arms flailing wildly above her head. She scrambled back to the house as fast as her feet would carry her.

By the time she entered the house, she was white faced and horrified. "My horse!" she panted. "My horse...has no ears!"

Trying to catch her breath, she looked up at her husband. Her eyes widened, and her mouth fell open. Then she screamed even louder. "AAAAAAAAAAAAAH! Your head! Look at your head!" she shouted and pointed with shaking fingers.

The farmer went over to the mirror and was horrified to find that his wish had come true. He was wearing the hat that his wife bought for her horse. He was also wearing the horse's ears and long black mane. "Oh, no! I got everything that was on the horse's head!" groaned the farmer.

"What has happened? What evil magic is this?" cried the farmer's wife. "Do something! Do something!" she screamed.

"I'll do something," said the farmer, "but in return, you must make a promise that you won't break."

"Yes, all right."

"If I can fix this, will you be nicer to me?"

"Yes, Yes."

"Will you fix nice meals sometimes and talk to me the way you talk to the horse?"

"Yes, Yes."

"And will you spend as much time with me as you do with the horse?"

"Yes, Yes! Anything! Just fix this mess!" And with that, she ran upstairs to sob into her pillow.

The farmer sat down to think. He stoked his long mane and pondered his situation. He thought that he had arranged a pretty good deal for himself. Unfortunately, he had no idea how to get the hat, horse ears, and horse mane off his head and back to the horse. He had used his one and only wish. He stayed up half the night thinking of a way to change the situation. Finally, as the oil lamps sputtered out, he said, "I've got it!" And with a smile, he went to bed.

Early the next day he went to the stone house that belonged to the magic toad. He turned over the stone and found the toad, its eyes flashing with anger at having been disturbed again. Then the toad saw the farmer's head and started laughing a deep croaking laugh.

"Heh croak heh! Look at you! I see you used your wish wisely. So, what do you want? I allowed you your one wish, and if you used it already, tough luck! We made a deal. You promised not to dig up my stone if I gave you a wish. You can't change that. Haw, haw, haw."

"I promised not to dig up your stone, but I didn't promise not to drop all the other stones I dig up on top of your stone. There are lots of stones in these fields, and I could bury your house under a very high pile of rocks if I wanted."

The toad knew this to be true. "Grrrrrrrrrrrrr! You are not an honorable man."

"That's true. And for that I'm sorry. But I'm also desperate."

"All right. I guess I'm stuck between a rock and a hard place."

"Huh?"

"Never mind. Look, if you promise never to harm my stone in any way, I'll give you one more wish."

The farmer was delighted to be given one more chance. "Deal! I wish to get rid of this horse mane, horse hat, and horse ears so my wife will keep the promise she made to me last night."

"Hey, wait a minute. That sounds like two wishes to me."

"But the two things are related. It doesn't seem fair that they should be separated into two different wishes."

"All right, all right. Look, I'll even throw in a third wish if you'll also wish to stop being such a whiner. No wonder your wife preferred whinnying to whining."

The farmer felt embarrassed to be called a whiner, but he persevered. "And I wish to stop whining," said the horse-eared man.

There was a strange and unfamiliar buzz around the farmer's head. It wasn't like the buzz that stable flies make. When the buzzing stopped, he reached up and felt his own ears again, and the hat and horse's mane were gone.

"Consider it done," said the toad. "But if you ever bother my stone again, I'll turn you into a horse so plagued by biting flies that you'll go insane." And with that, the toad slammed the large stone back onto the ground and was never seen again.

When he got home, the farmer opened the door. He smelled something. "I'm home," he called hesitantly.

To his surprise, the farmer's wife greeted him with a hug and said, "I thought I'd make a nice turkey dinner with all the trimmings for supper tonight."

"What about your horse?" asked the farmer.

"Oh, he's okay. I gave him a bag of oats. Now let's sit down and enjoy our meal."

Everything seemed too good to be true so the farmer decided to test his wife. "What do you say about me taking the horse out to the fields tomorrow to help with the work?"

He expected the usual berating from his wife, but instead she merely said, "Well, we all have to earn our keep on the farm, don't we?" Then she added, "Don't you think we should have some children, dear?"

"Well, yeah, sure. And I also think we should have a very good farming year," he said to his wife. His conversation was a little stale from lack of practice, but at least he wasn't whining.

"Here, dear," his wife offered, "have some more garden vegetables. You need to keep up your health. Oh, and don't forget your new hat tomorrow. It's going to be sunny all day."

# Jack Daw and
# Joe Crow

# Jack Daw and Joe Crow

## by Warren Rogers

——————————O——————————

Every morning, just before the sun peeked over the horizon, Jack Daw and Joe Crow bounced from branch to branch squawking and cawing loudly, in the tree beside Mr. Grundy's bedroom window.

"GET UP! CRAW! CROAK!

SUN'S UP! CAW! SKROAK!

WAKE UP! CAW-CRAW-CRAWWWWK!"

Every morning, Mr. Grundy exploded from his bed, untangled himself from his bedclothes, leaned out his window, shook his fist at the tree, and yelled, "Pipe down, you stupid birds!"

And every morning, Jack Daw and Joe Crow cawed back, "Pipe down, you stupid birds!"

Mr. Grundy yelled back, "Shut your black beaks."

So Jack Daw and Joe Crow cawed, "Shut your black beaks!"

Every morning, Mr. Grundy got so mad that he stomped up and down, and waved his fists while his face turned lobster red and his eyes almost popped out of his head. Mr. Grundy fumbled into his tattered robe, stormed to the bathroom, slammed the door, and muttered under his breath, "One of these days, I'll catch you two. Then you'll be sorry."

Old Mr. Grundy had been a grump for years. Since retirement he had been grumpy. When his wife died, he got grumpier and moved out of town so he could be alone. Now with Jack Daw and Joe Crow living in the woods near Mr. Grundy's house, and waking him up every morning at sunrise, Mr. Grundy is grumpier than ever.

Mr. Grundy was always stewing about Jack Daw and Joe Crow. "Some day I'm going to catch those feathered fools. And when I do, that'll be the end of them," he muttered to himself.

Mr. Grundy hated waking up in the morning because he had nothing to do. His house needed cleaning but he wouldn't clean it. His old black beat-up truck was rusty and dirty. It rattled and squeaked and backfired but he wouldn't fix it. Mr. Grundy just didn't care. His grass needed cutting. Weeds grew everywhere. Junk was scattered all over his yard. But Mr. Grundy didn't care. He didn't feel like doing anything. And the less Mr. Grundy did, the grumpier he became.

One fine morning, just before sunrise, Jack Daw and Joe Crow bounced from branch to branch in the tree beside Mr. Grundy's window and squawked and cawed every bird-word and noise they knew.

"GET UP! CRAW! CROAK!

SUN'S UP! CAW! SKROAK!

WAKE UP! CAW-CRAW-CRAWWWWK!"

And just as he did every morning, Mr. Grundy hung out his window in his pajamas, shook his fist at the tree and yelled, "Pipe down, you stupid birds!"

And Jack Daw and Joe Crow cawed back, "Pipe down, you stupid birds!"

Then Mr. Grundy yelled, "Shut your black beaks."

Jack Daw and Joe Crow cawed back, "Shut your black beaks!"

Mr. Grundy slammed down his window and muttered, "I'm going to get those feathered fools."

Then, as they did every morning, Jack Daw and Joe Crow flew off to hunt and scavenge for their breakfast.

Jack Daw and Joe Crow loved to eat. They didn't care if their food was a bug or a burger, a slug or a sandwich, or a worm or a waffle. Jack Daw and Joe Crow loved to eat just about everything.

But what they really liked best were wieners. It didn't matter what kind of wieners. Fat wieners, skinny wieners, brown wieners, red wieners, big wieners, little wieners, fresh wieners, stale wieners, juicy wieners, dry wieners, spicy wieners, bland wieners, long wieners, short wieners, beef wieners, pork wieners, wieners in a bunch or wieners on a string, they liked wieners more than anything!

As he did every morning, Mr. Grundy sat at his kitchen table, mumbling and grumbling as he read the newspaper and drank bitter black coffee. When he finished the paper, Mr. Grundy phoned the local radio talk show to complain about everything he didn't like. He had no one to talk to so he always phoned the radio talk shows and complained about everything and anything.

Then, just as he did every morning, Mr. Grundy walked outside, squinted up at the sky, and cursed about Jack Daw and Joe Crow under his breath. Mr. Grundy kicked at the pieces of junk in his yard and sauntered to the mailbox at the end of his driveway.

"Aha," said Mr. Grundy as he pulled out a special delivery brown envelope. "It's here!"

Mr. Grundy had been waiting two weeks for a very special recipe he had heard advertised on the radio.

Mr. Grundy thought back to how he found out about this special recipe.

Two weeks earlier, he was slumped in his dirty old armchair listening to his radio. Suddenly, a commercial yelled out at him:

**"Are you tired of the same old boring food every day? Well, wake up those taste buds with <u>Wiener-ama Deluxe</u>!**

**Yes, <u>Wiener-ama Deluxe</u>! The new recipe for those who aren't afraid to cook the best.**

**This award-winning recipe is guaranteed to please the most persnickety eaters.**

**Here's a meal that all will enjoy. The texture! The taste! The aroma!**

**Write today for your recipe. Just send $9.95, plus $3.00 for shipping and handling, to <u>Wiener-ama Deluxe</u>, 555 Fancy Food Way, Wiener Town, Washington.**

**Don't delay, write today!"**

Mr. Grundy wrote a cheque for $12.95 and sent away for the recipe immediately. He knew how much the crows loved wieners, and he had a plan.

Mr. Grundy hated to spend money, but he said to himself, "It's worth it if it'll help me catch those stupid birds."

Now, as he opened the brown envelope, he thought, "Things are going to be very different around here from now on."

In order to make Wiener-ama, Mr. Grundy had to take his beat-up truck into town, and buy twenty dollars worth of food and spices. Normally he got really mad if he had to spend extra money, but he kept thinking, "It's worth it if it'll help me catch those two beaked bozos."

When he returned to his run-down house, Mr. Grundy spent the rest of the day in the kitchen. He hated to cook but he said to himself, "It's worth it if it will help me catch those noisy noodle heads."

Mr. Grundy cut and chopped and ground up different kinds of meat. He added all sorts of smelly spices. He slowly fried the meats and spices and then drained the grease into an old can. He packed the fried mixture into wiener skins and tied up the ends. He put the wieners into a dish with a secret vegetable, fruit, and peanut butter sauce. Then he baked the wieners in the oven for four hours.

It was more work than Mr. Grundy thought it would be, but he reminded himself, "It's worth it if it helps me catch those two crummy crows."

Finally, the wieners were cooked.

Mr. Grundy put on two dirty oven mitts and pulled open the oven door. A thick, greasy, brown cloud of smoky steam poured from the oven. Mr. Grundy reached in and grabbed the hot baking dish. He thumped it on the counter and lifted the lid.

There they were—two of the hot-doggy-est, frank-furty-est, plump-juicy-est, taste-tempting-est wieners that anyone had ever seen or smelled. Mr. Grundy had created Wiener-ama Deluxe!

He put the cover back on the dish and glanced around the kitchen. What a mess! It looked as though there had been a food fight, or maybe a food war! Stuff was splattered everywhere.

Wherever he looked, Mr. Grundy saw greasy globs of goo hanging from the ceiling and walls. Milk, flour, ketchup, and pepper were splattered all over the kitchen cupboards and counter tops. Tomatoes were smashed into the cupboards. A white river of milk flowed across the floor to the basement stairs. There, a white waterfall carrying little specks of black pepper trickled down to a pool of milk on the basement floor.

A sticky brown sauce was hardening all over the top, side, and front of the white stove. Somehow, large rings of onion had been flung up into the kitchen light and fried on the hot bulb.

Leftover meat, vegetables, and sauces sat in dirty pots and pans piled up on top of each other on the counters and the stove, in the sink, on the refrigerator, and on the floor.

"Good," nodded Mr. Grundy as he stood in the kitchen doorway, "lots of food left for tomorrow's dinner." He switched off the kitchen light and went up to bed.

The next morning was not like all the other mornings. Yes, Jack Daw and Joe Crow squawked and crowed as the sun rose. Yes, Jack Daw and Joe Crow woke up Mr. Grundy with all their noise outside his window. But this morning was different. Mr. Grundy didn't yell at Jack Daw and Joe Crow, "Pipe down, you stupid birds!"

"Today will be a special day," smiled Mr. Grundy. "I'm going to catch those blasted birds with my Wiener-ama Deluxe."

When Jack Daw and Joe Crow flew off to find some food, Mr. Grundy clambered onto the roof to set his trap. He set down a big wire cage. Inside the cage were two specially made Wiener-ama Deluxe wieners. They were so spicy, so juicy, and so savoury that no crow would resist them. Then, he hid on one side of his roof, holding string that was attached to the cage on the other side.

It didn't take long for Jack Daw and Joe Crow to spot the wieners on the roof of Mr. Gundy's house.

"Hot Dog!" squawked Jack Daw.

"Hot Dog!" cawed Joe Crow. And down they flew. Luckily, they didn't see Mr. Grundy on the other side of the roof.

As the crows took their first delicious bite of wiener, Mr. Grundy pulled the string and the cage snapped shut.

"Gotcha!" crowed Mr. Grundy, with a mean look in his eye and an ironic tone in his voice. He said, "Don't worry, Mr. Grundy will take care of you."

"Don't worry, Mr. Grundy will take care of you," repeated Jack Daw and Joe Crow as they gobbled up their wieners.

"That'll be the last thing you mangy birds repeat," Mr. Grundy thought, "because I'm taking you to the garbage dump, and you can sit there in your cage and rot until you're nothing but feathers and bones!"

The thought of finally getting rid of Jack Daw and Joe Crow made old Mr. Grundy almost cheerful. Of course, Jack Daw and Joe Crow were always cheerful. They never thought that anyone would want to hurt them.

Mr. Grundy mumbled as he loaded the birds into the truck. "I don't care how long the drive is," thought Mr. Grundy. "It'll be worth it to be rid of these black-bozos forever."

It was a long drive to the garbage dump, and Mr. Grundy had to go through town to get there. As he drove he hummed to himself.

Not far down the road, Mr. Grundy came upon a young boy walking with an armload of books. Usually if Mr. Grundy was driving and he saw someone on the road, he honked his horn and hollered: "Get out of my way, you fool!" But because he had caught Jack Daw and Joe Crow, Mr. Grundy was feeling generous. Besides, he saw that it was Christopher, the boy from a nearby farm. Mr. Grundy sometimes bought rotten eggs from Christopher, to throw at Jack Daw and Joe Crow. Mr. Grundy stopped his truck.

"Hey, kid, you want a ride to school?" grunted Mr. Grundy.

Christopher knew not to take rides from strangers, but he knew Mr. Grundy. Everyone recognized Mr. Grundy's beat-up old black truck because he had honked at and yelled at everyone at some point.

"Yeah, thanks," Christopher said. "Usually it takes me two hours to walk to school. I'm always late. My teacher will be surprised...."

"I don't want to hear a long story," snapped Mr. Grundy. "If you want a ride, jump in."

"Don't worry, Mr. Grundy will take care of you," squawked Jack Daw and Joe Crow from their cage.

"Those are pretty smart crows you have," Christopher said to Mr. Grundy.

"Hmphfff," grunted Mr. Grundy.

"Where are you taking them?"

"I'm, uh…er, none of your business, kid." Mr. Grundy changed the subject. "Hey, why can't you get a ride to school if you live so far away?"

"The school bus broke down, and then the driver moved away."

"So ride your bike to school, kid."

"I do sometimes, but the roads get muddy when the weather is too cold and rainy," said Christopher.

"Hmmmm, kids these days," thought Mr. Grundy.

"Don't worry," cawed Jack Daw and Joe Crow, "Mr. Grundy will take care of you."

Mr. Grundy had had enough. He thought about how quiet his mornings would be after he dumped the birds on the garbage heap.

He soon came upon two other children who were walking along the road.

"Hey! There's Lewis and Lisa," said Christopher. "Will you stop for them, too?"

Mr. Grundy started to say, "Look, kid, why should . . ." but changed his mind and said, "Aw, well...I guess so."

Mr. Grundy's neck started to sweat. Ever since Mr. Grundy was a boy, his neck sweated whenever he felt nervous. It was against his grumpy nature to help anyone. But he stopped his truck anyway.

"I'm Mr. Grundy," he said as he wiped his neck with his handkerchief. "I'm taking your friend Christopher to school. You two might as well jump in, too."

"Thanks!" said Lewis and Lisa.

"Hey," exclaimed Lewis as they got in, "what are you doing with these neat crows?"

"Huh? Oh, uh, just taking them for a ride," Mr. Grundy lied. "They get tired of flying." Mr. Grundy didn't want to talk about the birds. He changed the subject. "I suppose you two are late for school every day as well, because you have so far to walk."

"Yes," replied Lisa, "Our teacher gets angry because sometimes we miss our lessons."

"Don't worry, Mr. Grundy will take care of you," Jack Daw and Joe Crow squawked.

The kids laughed when they heard the two crows speak, but Mr. Grundy only thought to himself, "Soon I'll be rid of these kids. Then I'll take the birds to the stinkiest, dirtiest part of the garbage dump. No one will ever find them."

As they drove along, the kids talked to and played with Jack Daw and Joe Crow. It was getting far too cheerful in Mr. Grundy's truck. Mr.

Grundy's neck was getting sweatier and sweatier. And his handkerchief was getting wetter and wetter.

The beat-up rusty black truck passed by two farms along the muddy, bumpy road. Just then, through the cracked and dirty windshield, Christopher spotted a young girl walking in the rain.

"Mr. Grundy, that's our friend, Jackie. Can we stop for her, too? Please?" Christopher pleaded.

Mr. Grundy had often seen Jackie at the store with her grandmother. He had known her grandmother when his wife was alive, and he had a bit of a secret soft spot for her.

"Oh, alright, alright," sighed Mr. Grundy. "I guess one more doesn't make any difference." He pulled the truck up beside the girl.

It was getting harder and harder for Mr. Grundy to be grouchy, but acting nice was making him really nervous.

"Come on in, Jackie," the kids shouted. "We're getting a ride to school today."

Jackie hopped into the truck. Mr. Grundy turned to her. "Look, kid, I know the story. You're always late for school, and you miss some of your lessons because you have to walk so far. So you can save your breath."

"Okay," said Jackie, "but it's still nice of you to give us a ride."

"Nice of me?!" Now Mr. Grundy's belly started to itch. His belly hadn't been itchy for years. It only got itchy when he was nice while he was trying to be mean. Mr. Grundy was really uncomfortable. But he still felt like being nice to these silly kids.

"Don't worry," Jack Daw and Joe Crow piped up, "Mr. Grundy will take care of you."

"Wow!" exclaimed Jackie. "Look at these beautiful birds. They're so black and shiny and funny. And they can talk, too! Where are you taking them?"

By now poor Mr. Grundy was steering his truck, wiping his wet neck, scratching his itchy belly, and trying to think of an answer.

"Huh?..The birds?...Oh, uh, I'm, uh, I'm just...." It was too much for Mr. Grundy. "Listen, kid," he shouted, "I'm just taking them out for a ride, you know, giving their wings a rest. Alright? Now, let me drive this thing and can the chatter, will ya?"

"Sure," said Jackie.

The kids didn't notice Mr. Grundy squirming, wiping, and scratching because Jack Daw and Joe Crow were so entertaining. The birds hopped and climbed and scrambled and hung upside down in the cage. They had beak fights. They made crazy noises.

"You guys are funny!" laughed the kids.

"You guys are funny!" Jack Daw and Joe Crow squawked back. Then they cackled like loony birds. Of course, this made Christopher, Lewis, Lisa, and Jackie laugh even more. Jack Daw and Joe Crow mimicked all the happy and silly sounds that the kids could think of. Mr. Grundy's truck was ringing with laughter.

"Pipe down, you stupid birds!" Mr. Grundy was going to yell. But all the laughter and merriment in Mr. Grundy's truck made him think. "Maybe those birds aren't so bad after all. Maybe."

And then...

BANG! RUMP-A-BUMP, RUMP-A-BUMP, RUMP-A-BUMP.

"Well, that's just great, isn't it?" Mr. Grundy said through clenched teeth as he stopped the truck.

"What happened?" asked Lewis.

"Well, what d'ya think happened, kid? The stupid, stinkin' dang tire blew out!"

From the back seat Jack Daw and Joe Crow squawked, "The stupid stinkin' dang tire blew out!" The kids giggled.

Mr. Grundy didn't giggle. He squeezed the steering wheel so hard that his knuckles turned white. His bushy old eyebrows furrowed, and his eyes began to bulge. His face started to turn lobster red, and his nostrils flared like an angry bull. He began to huff and puff and snort.

In the sparking, pumping, red light of his anger, Mr. Grundy wanted to grab the cage. He wanted to shake it and roar, "SHUT YOUR BLASTED BLACK BEAKS!" He saw himself throw the cage onto the road, jump back into his truck, and stomp on the gas pedal. He heard the engine roar. He jammed the truck into gear. He aimed the truck at the birds. He sped toward the birds in the cage. And then...and then...

"Can you fix it, Mr. Grundy? Can we help?" Lisa asked, interrupting Mr. Grundy's thoughts.

"Huh?" Mr. Grundy's eyes were returning to normal. "What's that?" His grizzly face changed from angry red to pink, then drained of color completely.

"I said," Lisa looked at him oddly, "can you fix the tire? Can we help you fix the tire?"

"I can fix it." He eyed the caged crows. "And you kids might as well help. You have to get out anyway so that I can jack up the truck."

"Jack up the truck," Jack Daw cawed.

"Jack up the truck," Joe Crow croaked.

The kids laughed and took the cage out of the truck and set it down behind a large rock.

Mr. Grundy murmured unpleasantly to himself and watched the kids play with the crows.

"Pardon?" said Christopher.

"Nothing. Hand me the jack," Mr. Grundy grunted.

Soon Mr. Grundy had the truck jacked and was removing the wheel. "Okay, kid, roll over the spare tire."

"Hey, what's that?" pointed Jackie.

Not far up the road a sickly looking brown animal walked drunkenly toward the truck, its head hanging low and its ears back.

"That looks like the Lawsons' dog," said Christopher. "but it looks kind of sick."

Mr. Grundy could see that the animal's fur was oily and matted. Its tongue dangled out the side of its frothy mouth. He could tell something was very wrong.

"Give me that tire. Quick! All you kids get back in the truck." Mr. Grundy's voice sounded strange. The kids got into the truck, except Jackie.

"I'll get the birds." She ran over to the big rock where she had set down the cage.

"No," yelled Mr. Grundy." With the wheel wrench in his hand he ran over to grab Jackie's arm.

By now, the strange dog was near the truck and making its way over to Mr. Grundy and Jackie.

"Get away!" Mr. Grundy shouted at the beast as he waved the wheel wrench at it.

The animal sniffed, then snarled as it approached Jackie. Mr. Grundy threw his wheel wrench at the beast, but missed. Quickly, he picked Jackie up and set her on top of the large rock. He turned to face the dog.

Although it was weak with sickness, Mr. Grundy could tell it was about to attack.

"Get out of here, you crazy dog," yelled the kids from the truck. They threw pencils, stones, books, rulers, and anything else they could find in the truck at the dog.

"Go on! Get!" they cried.

The animal turned quickly and charged toward the truck, snapping and growling wildly. The kids rolled up the windows and locked the doors. The enraged dog leapt up and rammed its slavering face into the truck window leaving gooey slobber all over it. Again and again it jumped and clawed at the side of the truck. Its bloodshot eyes were red with sick fury. The kids were scared, but they knew they were safe inside the truck.

Jackie and Mr. Grundy, however, were not safe. The dog turned back to them. With its eyes on Jackie, it flattened its ears and raised its hackles. It curled its lips back, revealing giant, sharp, yellow teeth. "AARR! ROWF! GRRR! NARG! GAR!" With a deep, low, growl it prepared to launch its attack. Mr. Grundy moved in front of Jackie. The kids in the truck stopped yelling. Jackie's throat was dry. The sick animal charged ahead.

Suddenly, from behind the big rock came the sound of loud fierce barks, growls, and snarls.

"AARR! ROWF! GRRR! NARG! GAR!"

The dog couldn't see who the noises were coming from, but it could tell that there were two of them. And they sounded large and fierce. Scared and defeated, the animal turned and ran across a nearby field into the bush.

"The stupid, stinkin' dang tire blew out!" squawked Jack Daw.

"Pipe down, you stupid bird!" cawed Jack Crow.

"Look," laughed Jackie as she watched the dog disappear into the bush, "your birds saved us!"

"I guess they did," whispered Mr. Grundy, shaken and pale.

"AARR! ROWF!" barked Jack Daw.

"GRRR! NARG!" snarled Joe Crow as the two birds flapped around in their cage behind the rock.

A short time later, as the grungy old truck pulled into the schoolyard, Christopher, Lewis, Lisa, and Jackie asked, "Mr. Grundy, would you bring your pet birds into the school to show our class?"

"Pet birds?! These aren't my..." Mr. Grundy started to say.

"Come on, Mr. Grundy. These crows are heroes. We have to show everyone," said Jackie.

Some of the good feelings that made Mr. Grundy so nervous had worn off, and he said, "Oh, alright, I guess it can't hurt."

Inside the classroom, Jack Daw and Joe Crow delighted the class with their antics and crazy noises. Meanwhile, Mr. Grundy watched as the kids told their classmates about the sick dog.

"We told the police about the Lawsons' dog," said Jackie. "The police said we were lucky the dog didn't bite anyone. They said they would go out and capture it. They thought it must have rabies."

The teacher thanked Mr. Grundy and said, "I hope all this hasn't made you too late for your appointment, Mr. Grundy."

"No," Mr. Grundy replied as he wiped his neck nervously, "I'm not too late, but I think I might skip it anyway." He was rethinking his plan to get rid of the birds.

"The children think you and your birds are very special, Mr. Grundy," said the teacher to a blushing, but pleased Mr. Grundy.

Mr. Grundy started to wipe the sweat off his neck, and he was about to scratch his itchy stomach when Jack Daw and Joe Crow squawked, "Don't worry, Mr. Grundy will take care of you!"

The students clapped, cheered, and whistled.

Mr. Grundy's neck was wet and his belly needed scratching, but there was the hint of a twinkle in his eyes.

Every morning since that day, just as the sun appears, Mr. Grundy wakes up to the voices of Jack Daw and Jow Crow.

"SKWAWK! CRAW! GET UP! SUN'S UP! SKROAK! CAW! CROAK! CRAWWWWWWWK!"

Mr. Grundy no longer hates the crows; he has even started to like them. He hangs out his window in his pajamas and calls, "Okay, okay already! I'm awake. Come down from your tree and get your breakfast— Wiener-ama Deluxe!

Jack Daw and Joe Crow are more like pets nowadays. Twice a week, Mr. Grundy cooks a new batch of Wiener-ama Deluxe. He no longer makes a mess in his kitchen.

Of course, Mr. Grundy is still angered by most things. He writes letters to the town newspaper grumbling about this and that, and he regularly phones the local radio talk show and complains about politics, taxes, and modern music.

But every second Saturday, Jackie's grandmother drives Christopher, Lewis, Lisa, and Jackie over to Mr. Grundy's house to visit Jack Daw and Joe Crow. They all have lunch, then, while the children spend the afternoon playing with the birds, Mr. Grundy and Jackie's grandmother sit quietly on the porch and sip tea.

# PLANKTON

# Plankton

## by Dave Leochko

The lakes and marshes of southern Ontario are surrounded by forests full of crunchy leaves and squirrels busily preparing for winter. Most animals are making last minute efforts to eat enough and find a place to sleep for the upcoming snowy season. Others like the Canada goose are preparing to head south for the winter.

Plankton the Goose was part of Flock number 132. The members of the flock had started preparations to head south as soon as they sensed it was cooling off after a stunning, boiling hot summer. Plankton's family—mom, dad, brothers and sisters, aunts, uncles, cousins, and grandparents—all stayed together to make the journey south.

Plankton and his family were having a difficult flight this year. It had become windy since they left northern Canada, and by the time they arrived in Ontario, they were all tired from facing harsh wind. Geese fly in a V pattern, with the strongest birds in the front of the V formation to cut the wind, making it easier for the weaker and younger birds to keep up. Head Goose guides the flock in the right direction so they land in familiar resting territory and finish their journey in the right place. Uncle Reed had been Head Goose for the past few days of the flight, and he was exhausted as they landed at a rest marsh

Plankton, at one and half years old, was just becoming an adult goose. He watched as Uncle Reed was comforted by his wife, and realized he would soon have to find his life-mate. For the moment he enjoyed being a young, carefree bachelor goose, chasing water bugs and playing with his friends. During this migration, all the others in his family were pressuring him to be Head Goose, but he was not interested in taking on such a big responsibility.

"Hey, Plankton," said Uncle Reed, "tomorrow you can take up the lead if you want."

Plankton did his best to ignore him, but knew that eventually he would have to grow up and take the lead. He was determined to wait as long as possible.

"Last year you were too young to take up the head, but now you're one of the strongest flyers, Plank. You should try it!" said his cousin Chestnut.

"Nah," answered Plankton, stretching his long neck to pick a tick out of his feathers. "Why would I want to do that? Uncle Reed knows where to go. Besides it's too much work. I like it at the back of the V."

Flying south was supposed to be fun, but this year it was turning out to be a real drag for Plankton.

"Hey, Chestnut—I just saw some picnickers on the other shore. You wanna waddle over there. They'll probably feed us, and then we can honk and hiss and flap our wings at the kids. I get a kick out of the way they run away scared. It's really funny."

"No, thanks," said Chestnut. He was doing his best this year to become responsible enough to head up Flock number 132.

Chestnut longed to be Head Goose. He could not understand why his cousin Plankton refused the honor. Chestnut was only going to be second in line this year

"Plank, Grandpa Bullrush saw a goose from Flock number 184. He told him he'd seen some ice on the lake already." Chestnut said.

"Oh...." Plankton was too busy thinking about playing with the picnickers to care about the flight and if there was ice on the water.

After two days rest, the family prepared for take off.

Grandpa Bullrush approached Chestnut and said, "Sorry, young Chestnut, but it's too windy and unpredictable for you to head up the V today, but you can be second in line if you want."

Disappointed, Chestnut said, "Okay, being second is still better than being at the back with all the little geese."

"Plankton, would you like to join Chestnut up front?" asked Aunt Waterlily.

"No, thanks, Aunt Waterlily. I like it back here," Plankton said casually. And he remained in his spot with the young geese at the back of the V.

The weather took a turn for the worse, faster than anyone anticipated. One day the flock had to fly through sleet. The icy rain stung their eyes. The lakes were starting to freeze. Open water was becoming harder to find, and the younger geese tired faster than the others so the family had to rest each day.

At the end of a particularly grueling day, they stopped at a small ice-covered lake.

"I'm sorry," said Uncle Reed. "I know there's no water around. We'll just rest for a few moments and then we'll move on."

Plankton was not happy. He had been pushed up to the middle of the V and had worked much harder than he was used to. He was very thirsty.

Uncle Reed started to round up the family. "We have to find a good sleeping spot." Plankton, however, began to wander around. He noticed a sign in the middle of the lake.

"DANGER! THIN ICE!"

Plankton was desperate for water, and he slipped away without anyone noticing. He ambled across the ice toward the sign where he could tell the ice was thin. He could still see the water underneath and began to peck away at the ice. After a few hard pecks, he heard cracking. He pecked until he made a hole large enough to drink from. Then he pecked and pecked until the hole was large enough to him to dip his feet in and sit for a while. Plankton shifted himself into the water. It was cold but a goose's feet don't get cold in the water. To Plankton, the water was relaxing and refreshing. "I should get back to the others," he thought. But he was very, very tired. "I'll close my eyes for just a minute."

Plankton opened his eyes to a crackling sound.

"Just the ice shifting," he murmured to himself, still half asleep.

As he became aware of his surroundings, Plankton also realized that it was dark, and he quickly woke up.

"Oh darn, it's nighttime," he said to himself, as he looked up at the starry sky.

"I better get back to the others," he thought. As Plankton flapped his wings, he realized he could raise his body, but could not move forward. He was stuck. The water had frozen around him!

"No problem," thought Plankton, as he tried to calm himself. "I'll just peck away at the ice again."

Unfortunately, while he slept, the temperature had fallen several degrees, and the ice was thicker than it had been earlier in the day. He honked as loud as he could to call the others. He was starting to panic.

His honk echoed across the silent blackness of the frozen lake.

No honk was returned. "Of course," realized Plankton. "They'll be gone by now."

While geese family members are close, they don't search for a lost member unless an emergency honk is heard. If someone is missing, the family assumes the missing goose has met up with a hunter.

"Nobody knows I slipped away earlier, I'm doomed," thought Plankton.

For most of the night Plankton tried to free himself. He was cold, miserable, and lonely. Snow started to fall as the poor goose grew exhausted and eventually fell asleep.

When he woke up, it was morning. Not too far away, he heard the sound of traffic. Still stuck in the ice, he turned his long neck around and saw a bridge with early morning traffic zooming over it.

Last night he had not really paid attention to where they had landed. Plankton now realized he was frozen in a lake in the middle of a city.

"Oh no!" thought Plankton. "My goose is cooked!"

Throughout the day, he noticed motorists laughing at him. Some people along the shore waved and yelled things at him. Some mean kids threw sticks and rocks at him, but luckily the shore was too far away.

"Not only am I done for," thought Plankton, "but this is such a humiliating way to go."

Night fell a second time, and he was still just as stuck as ever. The ice grew thicker as it got colder and darker. Plankton's hopes of rescue faded with the daylight. He was starting to feel the cold and he was hungry and thirsty. Plankton wondered where his family was. He thought they must be far south by now. With images of beaches and palm trees in his head, he finally dozed off.

Plankton woke to morning light and an unfamiliar sound. He looked over and saw a loud machine roaring toward him. He had never seen a snowmobile before, but he recognized that there were people on top of it.

"They're coming to get me," he thought. "It's no use even trying to frighten them, they'll just pull out their long sticks and boom! That'll be it for me." The men jumped off the machine and approached Plankton, not with guns, but with axes!

"This is worse," he thought. "They're going to chop me up right here and now!" Instead, the men started to chip away at the ice around Plankton.

"Of course," thought Plankton. "They have to free me before they can cook me." He could feel the ice around his feet moving, and he managed to pull himself free!

Plankton was so scared and confused that he didn't know what to do. He started slipping and sliding around the ice. He was ready to take off but his wings were covered in ice and snow. He couldn't fly.

"Well, will you look at that silly goose?" said the man in the big puffy parka. "He doesn't know which way to turn."

"I am not a silly goose," thought Plankton. Once more he slid on the ice and landed with a thud.

"Maybe I am a silly goose, after all," he thought. "Even if I could fly, I wouldn't know which way to go. I should have paid more attention to Uncle Reed."

"Well, Bruce, this bird is done for if we don't do something. Let's take it to the animal shelter," said the man in the big fluffy parka.

The two men took out a net and captured Plankton. He did not put up a fight. He knew that whatever lay ahead was his own fault.

They took Plankton to an animal shelter where he was placed in a cage. He was given food and was cared for. He overheard some kind people say the shelter was going to be his home for the winter months, and he would be released in the spring.

While Plankton liked the people who cared for him, they were nothing like being with his own family. His family were all enjoying the warmth of a fresh lake way down south.

Plankton became very sad. "I don't know where my family is; I have nowhere to go. What kind of life will I have on my own?" he thought to himself.

Winter slowly turned to spring. Finally, the day came for the shelter workers to free Plankton. He was placed inside a large crate and carried out to a waiting truck. After a bumpy ride, the crate was set down on the shores of a lake. The door opened, and he waddled slowly out toward the water. He looked back at the workers.

"Hey, I think that goose is going to miss us," said one of the men.

Plankton swam around for a long time, enjoying the water and fresh food, yet he still did not know what to do. As he swam around he noticed a bridge—it was the same bridge he had seen when he was stuck in the ice. He had been brought back to the same lake where he had spent those cold lonely nights in the ice last fall. It looked so different in the springtime.

"Well, since I know no other place, I may as well make this spot my new home," he thought.

The days went by, and Plankton grew accustomed to his new home. But still something was missing. One day, when he was sitting among the weeds, he saw the familiar V formation of geese overhead, honking one another. Plankton knew he could not just go up and ask if he could join a strange family.

Later that day, another flock flew by.

"Gee, this must be a popular flight route," thought Plankton. Then he remembered that geese always fly the same flight pattern. There *was* hope that his family would cross back over that lake on their way north. "Maybe that's why the shelter workers returned me here," he thought. "They sure know a lot about geese…for humans."

At that very moment, he heard a very familiar honking sound. He stretched his neck toward the sky. Above him was the familiar V pattern of his very own family—Flock number 132! Plankton rose up into the air toward the V.

"Plankton!" they called out.

"We never thought we'd see you again, " said Grandpa Bullrush.

"Join in," added Uncle Reed. "There's room for you in your usual spot."

"Actually, I think I'd like to be up front, if you don't mind," replied Plankton. He moved to the second spot in line and looked ahead to see Chestnut leading the flock.

"So what happened to you, Plank?" Chestnut called back.

"It's a long, long story. I'll tell you later, and one day I will share it with my children." said Plankton. His wings were weak but he flapped hard to keep his place in the V formation. The gaggle headed back, family intact, to their home up North.

# The Feed Me Fire

# The Feed Me Fire

## by Warren Rogers

*When Jupiter's bright and low in the sky*
*And Mars glows red like an angry eye*
*Be careful this night for you may hear*
*The goblins about and very near.*

**M**organ looked into the big pot on the stove. "Yuck. I hate this stuff."

"Aw, you girls always say that about my soup," Dad said, somewhat annoyed.

"Well, that's because it always tastes yucky," said Hartley.

His feelings hurt, Dad stomped out of the kitchen, letting the screen door slam for effect.

"He's not really mad, is he, Mom?"

"No, but it wouldn't hurt to give his soup a try," Mom said good-naturedly, even though she agreed with the girls. "When we come out to the cottage, making soup is fun for your dad. It's one of the few ways he can relax."

"Why can't he go fishing or bird-watching like other fathers?" asked Hartley.

"Or take cooking lessons so we can all relax?" volunteered Morgan.

They all laughed and were glad that Dad was out of earshot.

Hartley and Morgan liked to go to the cottage. They liked the swimming and hiking, the horseback riding, the gardening, and the bug collecting. They also loved to have an evening campfire.

"Can we stay up for a fire tonight, Mom?" asked Hartley.

"Yeah, can we, Mom? Please?" pleaded Morgan.

"Sure. I guess that'll be okay."

They loved to stay up late to see the stars and planets and watch for satellites and meteors. They played Tag and Hide and Seek in the shadows of the trees and bushes around the cottage. In early summer, the fireflies flashed codes to one another. Dad said they were fairies talking to one another. The girls liked to believe this.

That night, as usual, Dad and Mom started the fire and brought out hot chocolate and marshmallows to toast on the campfire. Hartley liked to toast hers golden brown. Morgan liked to set hers on fire, then blow them out and bite through the crispy, thin, black layer into the sweet melted center. All the while, they took turns telling stories.

When they finished their marshmallows, the girls searched for dead twigs to keep the fire going. The stars glittered in the black summer sky.

"Hey, Morgan, do you think the sky looks kinda different tonight?" Hartley asked.

"I dunno, I guess it looks kinda . . . thicker. Sort of dark and 'gluey'. Do you smell something funny?"

Both girls sniffed at the air.

"That's probably just the fire," said Hartley.

Morgan always liked to find Jupiter in the sky before anyone else. "There's Jupiter," she pointed out triumphantly.

"You're right," Dad said. "And there's Mars over there." He pointed to the reddish star. "It looks really red tonight. Hey, you know what my grandma used to say, don't you girls?"

"No, what?"

"Now, dear," cautioned their mom, "don't go scaring the girls."

"Let's see...how did it go...? Oh yeah:

> 'When Jupiter's bright and low in the sky
> And Mars glows red like an angry eye
> Be careful this night for you may hear
> The goblins about and very near'."

"Ooooo!" Morgan hunched over and shivered. "She said that?"

"Nice going," whispered Mom, as she elbowed Dad.

"Well, yeah, but it was just to get us kids to go to bed."

"Oh," said Morgan, reassured.

Hartley looked up at the sky. The stars seemed to be colder, and they glinted like the edges of broken glass. Something was different. She felt nervous. The branches on the old maple looked more than ever like scary fingers reaching out. The girls always talked about the maple tree's 'scary hands'. In the darkness, the large rocks seemed like angry toad heads rising out of the ground. On a normal night, she would have tried to scare Morgan, but on this night she decided she had better not. Instead, she started playing their regular game of 'feeding the fire'.

"Here you go, fire," one of them would say.

"Thank you," the other one would answer for the fire.

"Here's a tasty one," one would say.

"Yummy," the other would answer.

As the girls fed the sticks to the fire, Dad said, "Be careful around the fire. Don't play with it. Just put the sticks on." A few minutes later, Mom said, "Don't stand in the smoke; you'll ruin your lungs."

But the game continued. Hartley placed a dead twig on the fire and said, "Here you go, fire."

A warm, flickering voice answered, "Thank you."

"Did you hear that?" Hartley squeaked.

"Yeah, that was you," said Morgan.

"No," she paused, "It wasn't."

"Well, who was it then?"

They looked over at Dad, but he was deep in conversation with Mom.

"Give the fire more sticks." It was the voice again.

Morgan snapped off a few dry twigs from the branch in her hand and threw them into the fire.

"Ahhh! Mmmm! Goood!" said the voice.

"It's the fire," they squealed with amazement. They squinted at it, and Morgan said, "You know, if I look at it a certain way, I can sort of see a face."

Hartley peered closely, then agreed, "A fire face!"

"I want more," the fire said.

"Did you hear what the fire just said?" the girls tried to get the attention of their parents.

Their parents smiled at each other. "No, we didn't hear anything. Sorry."

Then Dad leaned over close to Mom. "Isn't that cute how the nighttime really gets the kids' imaginations working overtime?"

Mom looked at him sideways. "Yes, the nighttime and someone else."

The girls were having the most magical time. "Did you say you want more?" asked Hartley.

"Yes, more," said the fire.

When Hartley put on a stick, the fire hummed strange musical notes and said, "M-m-m-m-more."

The girls were delighted. "This is fun! What a great game!" They ran around in the dark with dancing flashlights and gathered sticks for the fire.

And each time they put more sticks on the fire, it said, "M-m-m-m... More!"

After a lot of running back and forth to the fire, the girls were exhausted. They stopped to rest.

"More!" said the fire.

"This isn't fun anymore. We're tired of this game," said Hartley, "We're going to stop."

"You will feed me!" the fire commanded.

"Nope. Sorry. Too tired."

"You will feed me, or I will burn down your house!" the fire said in a dry hissing way that sounded really scary.

The girls looked at each other nervously. Then they said, "All right. But just until we have to go to bed." The girls continued to search for sticks, and their parents continued to chat until finally announcing "Girls. It's time for bed."

The girls threw their sticks on the fire and said, "We have to go to bed now, Fire. Good night!"

"You will continue to feed me!" ordered the fire.

"But we can't, we have to go to bed now."

The fire flared up and roared, "You will feed me, or I will burn down your house!" Inside the fire, the girls saw an image of their house burning. Then the fire spat hot sparks and spewed smoke at them.

"C'mon, kids, let's go," Mom called.

Hartley and Morgan didn't move from the fire; their faces were full of anxiety. "Don't worry girls," Dad said. "I'll make sure the fire's completely out. I've got the water hose right here." He thought they were being uncharacteristically concerned.

The girls reluctantly went to their bedroom, but they watched intently from the upstairs window as their father doused the fire with water.

"Oh no," they both gasped as a great cloud of angry steam rose into the air and formed an angry face that glared straight at them before it floated off.

Later, when everyone was in bed, the girls lay awake nervously waiting for something to happen. They took turns going to the window to check the fire pit. Each time they checked, the fire pit was lifeless. Finally, when the girls were confident that the fire had gone out for good, they fell asleep.

No sooner had they drifted off in a restless sleep than a noise woke them up.

"Did you say something?" whispered Morgan.

"No, did you?" answered Hartley.

Then they heard it, "Feed me!"

They both ran to the window. They saw the fire pit glowing red. It was pulsing—bright, dim, bright, dim—like a beating heart.

The voice seemed to be talking right inside their heads. "Feed me or I'll burn your house down." And to show it meant what it said, the goblin fire shot out long flames toward their window and then, just as quickly, brought its fiery arms back and clapped them together, sending a shower of sparks high into the night sky.

"What'll we do?" whimpered Hartley. "We can't just keep feeding it. It's turning us into its slaves."

"Let's go tell Mom and Dad," suggested Morgan.

Hartley shook her head. "They're not going to believe us."

But Morgan ran into their parents' bedroom and shook their bed. "Mom! Dad! The fire is awake, and it says it's going to burn down our house!"

"I told you they stayed up too late," yawned Dad.

"And I told you not to tell them your grandmother's scary stories," Mom said to him. "It's just a bad dream, Morgan. You can come in our bed if you want."

"No, the fire's not out. It's glowing red!" insisted Morgan.

"Honey, go check the fire." said Mom.

"Oh, all right," Dad sighed. He got out of bed and went to the window. All he could see was darkness. "There's no glow. It's out, girls. C'mon. I'll take you back to bed."

He tucked them in. "Now, let's not have any more bad dreams, okay?" He left.

"I told you they wouldn't believe you," whispered Hartley. The two girls lay quietly in the ominous darkness, listening. For a time, all was quiet. But soon, outside their window, they heard the distinct sharp snapping, crackling sounds of a blazing fire.

"It's the fire," Hartley breathed. "We'll have to feed it until we make a plan."

The girls had no choice but to go out and feed the fire more sticks. It was very dark and the air hummed with hungry mosquitoes. It wasn't long before Morgan and Hartley were exhausted. The fire insisted that they keep feeding it.

"Morgan, go turn on the water, and I'll spray the fire." Her sister did so, but when Hartley aimed the hose at the fire, the water instantly changed to steam even before it reached the flames. And the hose got so hot that it started to burn her hands. She yelped and let go as the fire chuckled low and mean.

"This is hopeless," she said of the hose.

"What are we going to do?" Morgan was exhausted.

"We'll have to find something that is poison to the fire."

They tried killing it with old rotten wood, but the fire ate it. They fed it old shingles from an outhouse roof, but the fire loved it.

"Delicious!" it said as flames licked the air. It roared bigger than ever and belched out thick curls of black smoke.

"Morgan, you keep feeding the fire some good dry sticks. I have an idea!" Hartely scurried away.

When Hartley returned she had the fire extinguisher hidden in her jacket. Morgan's face was covered with scratches and mosquito bites, and she was sobbing weakly.

Hartley pulled out the fire extinguisher and yelled, "Eat this! You mean, greedy fire!" She aimed the extinguisher at its base. But when she squeezed the trigger, the fire snarled as the extinguisher's foam oozed like melting wax and dripped uselessly at her feet.

The fire flared up and set a shrub on fire. Hartley screamed and turned the fire extinguisher on it, smothering the fire and saving the house from going up in flames.

"Let that be a lesson to you," the fire crackled with mean laughter.

In all the excitement, Morgan snuck back to the kitchen and came running back, carrying the large pot of her dad's homemade soup. She ran up to the laughing fire, tripped, and landed just in front of it. The pot of soup sailed into the air and spilled all over the greedy fire.

Hartley helped Morgan up.

They stared as the angry fire bellowed its disapproval and hissed in sick steamy agony. Then it moaned and whimpered and shrunk into a small black bubbling pool of sludge...until it was no more.

The girls looked at each other, then back to where the fire had been. They waited. The mosquitoes whined in their ears, and bit their arms, but the fire remained quiet

Back in their bedroom, they kept an eye on the blackened fire pit, still unconvinced that the fire was dead. Finally, just as dawn approached, the two exhausted sisters fell into a deep sleep.

At breakfast, two bleary-eyed girls smelling of smoke and covered with bright red mosquito bites entered the kitchen.

Mom gasped. "You children look terrible. You both look like smoked fish!"

"Well, I told them not to get too close to the fire last night," Dad said. He opened the fridge. "Hey, all of my homemade soup is gone. I'd better make another batch." He made a mental note to find the onions, jam, and chili sauce.

Instead of gagging, the girls looked at each other, "Good idea, Dad. It's always good to have some of your soup around. You never know when you might need it."

"Well, thanks, kids. See," he said to his wife. "I told you they would come to appreciate my soup-making skills!"

# I Remember When

# I Remember When

## By Dave Leochko

An old man and a young boy sat on a bench in the garden behind the old man's home. The garden was a beautiful place for the residents of the Shady Lanes Seniors' Home to escape the sterile smells of their rooms and the colorless white uniforms of the staff.

In the garden, chattering squirrels and chirping birds broke the serenity. Blossoms and flowers blended to create a wonderful fragrance.

The old man and the young boy had sat here every day for a week, sometimes in silence, occasionally speaking. The two stared at the carefree squirrels playing on the lawn.

"I remember Momma taking me to the park for the first time when I was little. I had a soother that I used to suck on all the time and would not give up. Momma said I was getting too big to need a soother."

A little while later, "I remember sitting with Momma watching the squirrels and then going to play on the swings. I left my soother on the bench, but when I came back, it was gone. I started to cry. But Momma came over and said the squirrels had probably taken it for their babies. Momma gave me a comforting hug. When I was older, I found my soother in Momma's purse. As it turned out, she—not the squirrels—had it all along."

"I'm sure she didn't mean to trick you, maybe it was the only way she could get it away from you without hurting you."

The two sat in silence, watching the squirrels nibble acorns.

"I remember how Momma could make all kinds of food to make me feel just right. I would crawl out of bed, come down for breakfast, and find scrambled eggs on my plate. I called them "snow eggies." They looked so light and fluffy, just like snow. Only Momma knew how to make snow eggies just right.

"I walked home for lunch every day even though Momma said I could stay at school with my friends. I didn't want to. As soon as I opened the door, I could smell what Momma was making. On cold winter days she made chicken noodle soup with little bits of wiener. It was the best soup ever. I liked to sit and read my book at the kitchen table while Momma got lunch ready and hummed to herself. Sometimes, I tried to figure out what song Momma was humming. Whenever I asked, she said it was just a song she had heard on the radio. Now when I hear those songs on the radio, I think about her humming while I ate my lunch.

"Whenever I was sick, Momma knew how to make me feel better. She made fancy little sandwiches with no crusts and cut into all kinds of shapes. She brought them out on a tray to where I was wrapped in a blanket, surrounded by all my favorite toys, on the sofa. I remember a lot about Momma."

Silence drifted over the duo once again.

"Come, let's walk around to the pond," suggested the old man in a somber tone. The two walked on the cobbled stones toward the pond. On such a hot afternoon, the water appeared translucent. The fountain gurgled as the water flowed through its pipes. Inside the pond, goldfish darted around.

"I remember when I wanted a dog, and Papa said no. He said pets belong on farms where they have room to run around. I cried myself to sleep that night, with my head in my pillow. During the night I felt Momma's hands on my head, stroking my hair. Momma's hands weren't soft, with fancy nail polish. They felt crispy, bumpy, and rough. Momma's hands had lots of lines on them. She called them 'dishwashing hands.' She said she didn't care—she had better things to do than worry about her hands. But Momma's hands were the best for patting your head. I could feel each bump as she laid her hand on my head.

"The next morning, sitting on my bureau, was a little glass bowl with two goldfish. When I came running out of the room, Momma smiled and said they weren't the same as a dog, but a pet is a pet no matter what. My Momma was a good Momma."

The old man and the boy sat in silence looking at the ground.

"Grandpa," the boy turned to the old man, "now that Momma is gone, will I forget her?"

"No, son, even though your Momma can't be here with you anymore, she will always be with you in your memories. She will never leave you."

"I'm glad I will always remember her" the young boy said. "Look, Grandpa, a frog!" Just then a frog hopped onto the cobblestones. It sat for a long time. Then it sprang into the long, tall grass off the path.

"I wonder what it's looking for," asked the young boy. "Let's follow it and find out."

# Rainy and the Lucky Cat Food

# Rainy and the Lucky Cat Food

## by Warren Rogers

———————————O———————————

Rainy lived in the woods separating the Modern World from Storybook World. Not so long ago, a servant from the Evil Queen's castle found a baby who had been abandoned. The servant named the baby Spring Rain and raised her with love and care. When the Evil Queen found out about the child, she dismissed the servant and adopted the young girl herself. The Queen was bored and thought it would be fun to have a daughter who she could yell at and boss around.

The name Spring Rain, though, sounded much too pleasant to the Evil Queen Mommy, so she renamed her Rainy. The Queen commanded that Rainy have no playthings or books, and no one was to teach her how to read or write. No one, not even the animals, was allowed to speak to Rainy. The Queen also decided that Rainy would wear only servant's clothes.

Once, a servant who felt sorry for Rainy talked to her. He even called her by her real name, Princess Spring Rain. The Evil Queen Mommy found out that the servant had disobeyed her, and he was never seen again.

The servants never talked to Rainy again. Just to be sure that Rainy didn't talk to anyone, the Evil Queen Mommy ordered all living creatures around the castle to move to another Storybook province, far far away. Big black insects and rats were allowed to stay, and they lived in the darkness beneath the castle. The Evil Queen Mommy liked the diseased rats and the scuttling chewing insects because they sent fear into the hearts of her servants. Storybook World was a bleak and sad place, and Rainy was miserable and lonely.

The Evil Queen's castle was located in an area of Storybook World that was right beside the Modern World. Evil Queen Mommy was able to get Modern World Cable TV (MWCTV). She spent all of her time loafing around watching her favorite shows. While she sat like a lump watching TV, she shouted orders to Rainy. Rainy had to do all the most horrible, dirty, and stinky chores.

One day, during a commercial break in her favorite soap opera, the Evil Queen summoned Rainy to her bedroom. She ordered her to clean the slimy gooey walls inside the old stone well in the courtyard.

Rainy quickly realized that scrubbing the slimy walls with a brush was not going to work. She was going to need a cleanser to cut through the grime. She didn't know what to do. She was afraid to ask the Evil Queen Mommy for anything. She would punish Rainy for interrupting her TV show.

After a few minutes. Rainy decided that her punishment would be worse if she didn't get the well walls crystal clean. She summoned up her courage, took a deep breath, and called up to the Evil Queen's window.

"Excuse me, your most magnificent majestic majesty?" This was a name she was forced to use when referring to the Queen.

There was no answer. She could hear the TV blaring through the window.

She tried again. "Excuse me, your most magnificent majestic majesty?"

Upstairs, the Queen was snacking on chocolate eclairs—her favorite Modern World food. She waited for a commercial, then flung off the bedcovers, scattering eclairs and potato chips all over the floor. She dragged herself out of bed and stomped over to the window.

"This had better be important, you little wart!" she yelled down from her window. "I'm busy."

"I need something to help me clean the inside walls of the well, your most magnificent majestic majesty," trembled Rainy.

"You'll need Star Bright Cleaning Detergent." The Queen knew about the detergent because she had just seen a commercial on television. "You'll have to go to the convenience store in the Modern World," said the Queen. She threw some money out the window. "Here's $20, but I'm going to count the change, so you had better not spend any on yourself. Don't even think about going anywhere but directly to the store and back."

"I won't, your most magnificent majestic majesty," Rainy mumbled.

She remembered the time she had tried to run away from the Evil Queen Mommy. When she was finally found, cold and starving, she was locked in the cellar of the castle for two weeks.

Rainy was glad for a chance to get away from the castle, even if it was just to go to the Modern World. She didn't much like the Modern World; it was messier and smellier than her Storybook World. Still, it was a break from the Queen's constant yelling.

She walked along the forest path until she came to a fork in the road. There were many signs pointing in different directions, including signs to the Big Bad Wolf's House and the Three Little Pigs' Place. Rainy couldn't read, but she knew the sign showing tall buildings was the path to the Modern World. She started down it.

As Rainy came to the edge of Storybook World, she stepped out of the lush green forest and into a concrete city filled with thick smelly brown air. She coughed as she crossed a street littered with blowing bits of trash. She spotted the convenience store right away, and weaved her way through the grimy cars to the door.

Inside the store, everything looked strange under the fake lights. She tried to figure out where she might find the cleanser. She noticed a rack of colorful, shiny papers and picked up a magazine.

"Hey, what do you think this is—a library?"

Confused, she said "What's a library?"

"Very funny," frowned the clerk behind the counter.

"I'm looking for Star Bright Cleaning Detergent.

"Yeah, well, it's at the end of this aisle beside the cat food. It's in the blue box with the yellow star..."

"Thanks," Rainy said, excited to have talked to someone other than the mean Queen back in Storybook World.

"...or is it the yellow box with the blue star?" the clerk muttered to himself.

Rainy reached the end of the aisle "Hmmm, let's see. There are yellow boxes with blue stars, and there are blue boxes with yellow stars. Did he say the yellow box with the blue star or the blue box with the yellow star? It must be this blue box because blue makes me think of water." She took the box up to the checkout counter and gave the clerk the $20.

"Here's your change," said the clerk.

"Thank you," replied Rainy, eyeing the boxes of candy beside the checkout counter. She longed to have a treat for the long walk home, but she knew the Evil Queen Mommy would count the change, and it had to be exact.

To make it all worse, she noticed a nice mommy buying treats for her daughters, and she began feeling very sorry for herself. She wished she had someone to watch over her and protect her. She sobbed as she walked back to the court of the Evil Queen. Whenever she went to the Modern World, she was sad because it reminded her of all the things she would never be part of.

When Rainy arrived back at the courtyard, she opened the blue box with the yellow star. She poured its contents onto her brush and started to scrub the inside walls of the well.

"Oh, no!" Rainy cried. "This isn't Star Bright Cleaning Detergent!"

To her horror, she realized she was spreading brown gooey cat food all over the stones.

"I've made a smelly, smeary mess! Oh, when Queen Mommy sees this, I'll be in terrible trouble! What am I going to do?" Rainy collapsed with her head in her hands beside the well and sobbed hopelessly.

While Rainy was crying with despair, the yellow star on the blue box of cat food started to glow. Then it began to shake. Then it began spinning faster and faster until it spun so wildly, it flew right off the box.

In a bright flash, a plump purple cat in a pink dress appeared in front of her. It reached out its paw and patted her on the back.

Rainy looked up in shock.

"Meow, meow, my rear."

"Huh?"

"I mean . . . Now, now, my dear. Excuse me, but I'm not used to using words."

"Wh- What are you? You look like a big purple cat in a pink dress."

"Why, yes, dear, I'm a Hairy Fat Mother...I mean...I'm a Fairy Cat Mother. I usually just help cats, but you are so lonely and sad that I thought I'd like to help you."

"How?" asked Rainy in disbelief, desperate for it to be true.

"If you do exactly as I say, everything will be all right. Will you trust me?"

"I—I guess so," stammered Rainy.

"Food curl...I mean...good girl." The cat leaned closer to Rainy. "Here's what we have to do."

Still unsure about this so-called Fairy Cat Mother, Rainy listened to her instructions. "Call the Queen down to the well to look at your work," the cat said.

"No!" choked Rainy, "I can't. If she sees this mess, she'll be enraged. Her punishment will be awful."

"Now, now, you can trust me. I'm here to help you, remember? You'll see everything will be okay," purred the cat.

Rainy hadn't yet had much luck in her life. Looking into the purple cat's eyes, however, she had a feeling she could trust her.

"Now," said the cat, "call the Queen, and ask her to come and inspect the well walls."

Rainy hesitated, then walked timidly toward the Queen's window. Nervously, she called, "Oh, your most magnificent majestic majesty?"

Nothing happened. Rainy looked back at the Fairy Cat Mother.

"Louder," whispered the Fairy Cat Mother.

Rainy tried again in a louder voice. "Excuse me, your most magnificent majestic majesty?"

This time, the Evil Queen's dark miserable figure appeared at the window.

"What do you want?" She snorted, "This had better be important, you little cockroach."

She scowled at Rainy. "Did you get the detergent?"

"Yes, your most magnificent majestic majesty."

"Did you spend any of the change on yourself?"

"No, your most magnificent majestic majesty."

"Did you clean the grimy well walls?"

Rainy was terrified to lie to the Queen. She knew the punishment would be unbearable. She looked at the Fairy Cat Mother for help.

"Tell her, 'Yes'."

Looking back up at the Queen, she mumbled, "Yes, your most magnificent majestic majesty."

"Tell her that you're freddy for a fin section," the cat whispered.

"I'm freddy for a fin section, your most magnificent majesty."

"You're WHAT?" roared the Queen.

"Oops. Tell her that you're ready for an inspection," said the Fairy Cat Mother.

"I'm ready for an inspection, your most magnificent majesty."

The Queen looked puzzled. "An inspection, huh?"

The Fairy Cat Mother whispered, "Tell her again. You must get her to come down here."

Rainy was so frightened she could barely blurt out the words. "Please come down, and see how clean I made the walls, your most magnificent majesty."

"Those walls had better be spotless, or I'll have you scrubbing out the stinking dungeons in the deepest, darkest, dankest part of my castle where the rats are as big as your leg."

Rainy gulped and shuddered. She knew the Evil Queen Mommy meant what she said.

The Fairy Cat Mother told her, "Ask again."

"Please come, and see what a good job I've done, your most magnificent majestic majesty."

"It had better be perfect!"

Rainy went back to the well to wait for the Queen. She looked at the grimy stone walls smeared with cat food and murmured, "What a mess!"

"Relax, child," purred the Fairy Cat Mother. From under her skirt, she pulled a long pink and orange ribbon with a flashlight attached to one end and said, "When the Evil Queen comes, give her this light so that she can look inside the dark well."

"Okay," said Rainy, "but what am I…" She looked around, but the cat had disappeared.

"Don't leave me!" cried Rainy.

The Evil Queen Mommy stomped up to the well. "What are you talking about?" She sneered, "I just got here."

The Evil Queen Mommy towered in front of Rainy. She stood on Rainy's toes and breathed foul breath down on her face. With watering eyes, Rainy looked up at the Queen. The Evil Queen thought Rainy was crying, and she smiled wickedly.

Rainy gathered her thoughts together and remembered the Fairy Cat Mother's instructions. She shook with fright as she handed the light to the Queen. "Here, your most majestic majesty."

"Get out of my way, you little toad!" the Queen grabbed the light and started to lean into the well to inspect the walls. She lowered the light into the well and screamed, "Ahhh! What is this? These walls are filthy! You little monster! I'm going to...Hey, this light is getting heavier! I can't let it go! It's too heavy! It's pulling me down! Nooooooo!"

Rainy watched in shock as the Evil Queen's skirt, legs, and feet disappeared into the well. She rushed over to the edge of the well just in time to see a bright flash at the very bottom. She retreated quickly as streams of colors from deep inside the well shot high into the sky. Their force knocked Rainy to the ground. From there, she watched the sky fill with colors swirling and spinning together into a giant ball of yarn. The ball exploded like dazzling fireworks in the sky.

At first, thousands of flower petals fell like snow. But they soon changed to colored cat treats that, like hailstones, bounced off everything. Rainy tried to catch some of the treats as they fell. With open arms, she was surprised when a tiny white kitten dropped from the sky and into her hands.

Just then, the Fairy Cat Mother reappeared.

"What happened to the Queen?" asked Rainy.

Quietly, the Fairy Cat Mother said, "She's gone. She'll never be mean to you again." She looked at the pure white kitten in Rainy's arms, and continued, "Beneath all the evil, the Queen Mommy did have some goodness deep within her. That bit of goodness remains." The Cat reached over and stroked the kitten's head.

With the Queen gone, Rainy changed her name back to Spring Rain, and she became Queen Spring Rain. With the magical help and wise advice from the Fairy Cat Mother, Spring Rain immediately started to make changes for the better. She was the most generous and kind monarch in Storybook World history. She cleaned out the horrid dungeons and sent the rats and bugs to servant training school. When the rats returned to the castle, they were hired to tend the castle's wine cellar. The many visitors to the castle were treated to delicious food and luxury service by an army of robed shiny black bugs.

Spring Rain changed the rest of the castle into a luxurious theme hotel, called Storybook Suites. Guests stayed in rooms decorated to look just like settings from their favorite stories. There were the *Dwarf's Kingdom*, the *Giant's Pantry*, the *Fairy's Forest*, the *Troll's Bridge*, and the *Rapunzel's Tower* suites along with many others.

In the dining room, visitors could eat tasty Storybook food such as *Jack Horner's pie, Humpty Dumpty's omelette, Mad Hatter's teas, Gingerbread Man's cookies, The Fox's Grapes,* and many other fantasy foods.

The grounds around the castle became popular with people from the Modern World and storybook characters alike. They hiked and had picnics and laughed and played all day long. Wildlife and forests were protected and grew and prospered all over Storybook World.

Spring Rain finally had the happy home she had always longed for, and she was never lonely again. She called the kitten Majesty and loved and cared for her. Majesty loved to sleep in front of the TV and display her rainbow-colored claws. She ate only cat food from the blue box with the yellow star. At night, Majesty curled up on her pillow beside Queen Spring Rain and purred until the two peacefully fell asleep.

# PART 5

# Beyond Literature Circles

# Beyond Literature Circles

Once the students have become comfortable with the Literature Circles process, you can adapt and modify it to use in other areas of the curriculum. Literature Circles can become an integral part of learning.

The process can be helpful in areas such as math, social studies, science, health, art, and poetry. Once students understand how to work well with their groups, and have acquired the skills to communicate effectively, they are ready to adapt the process in other curriculum areas. With any curriculum, the Literature Circles process creates a forum for closer examination and deeper appreciation and understanding of material. By holding structured discussions, students confirm their thoughts, are exposed to other views, and are able to learn from one another.

As we transition to other parts of the curriculum we aim to keep the process intact. We maintain regularly scheduled discussions, preparation time, and planning time.

Students read assigned articles or work on problems by themselves prior to meeting. When they assemble in their groups, students are prepared to discuss the problem or article, show how they worked with it or solved it, and discuss what difficulty they might have had in solving it.

We have recently worked the Literature Circles methodology into Math Circles, Poetry Circles, Art Circles, and Music Circles. Following are a few examples that have worked well for us in these areas.

## Math Circles

Math Circles and Literature Circles share the same goal—to provide a forum in which students learn from others. Unlike Literature Circles, Math Circles do not last very long. To allow students the opportunity to choose their own problem, create a variety of problems for them to look at. As with Literature Circles, students should be introduced to a number of problems and should be given the opportunity to choose. Once the students have each selected their problem, the groups are formed.

Each student takes the problem and tries to solve it on his or her own before the group meets to talk about it. Have students fill in their role sheet while they are working on their problem.

On their role sheets they should explain what the problem is, preferably in their own words. This is a challenge that re-enforces how important it is for students to be able to clearly articulate different kinds of issues. When the group comes together, students find it interesting to see how others interpreted the problem.

While tackling the problem, students should consciously remember all of the problem solving skills they have learned and use the one that best suits what they are working on. Students should record how they solved the problem on their worksheet.

Once each member of the group has completed the problem, the students should assemble in their group to compare answers and strategies. They determine if there is more than one answer, and then discuss which is correct. The discussion allows stronger math students to explain concepts and ideas to the others. Sharing in the Math Circle allows students to see the different ways in which people interpret problems. Students learn other strategies that they might use in the future. The atmosphere can be exciting for students. Learning outcomes are also met because students tend to retain much of what they learn in Math Circles.

## Sample Math Problem for Math Circles

Josh was hungry. He decided to make himself a midnight snack. He was just about to open the fridge when, suddenly, the lights went out. In the darkness, he had to rely on his memory to locate the different food jars in the fridge.

Read what Josh remembers. Then label each jar in the picture.

1.  The mustard, syrup, and pickles are all in jars of different sizes, and on different shelves.

2.  The syrup and pickles are on the left side of the fridge. The syrup is below the pickles.

3.  The mustard, jam, and soup are all in small jars.

4.  The jam shares the shelf with the syrup. All sweet stuff are on this shelf.

5.  The milk is next to another dairy product.

6.  The ketchup is on the top shelf. It is not the same size as either the pickles or the soup. The juice can be found next to the ketchup.

7.  The relish is between the milk and mustard.

8.  The honey is the biggest jar on its shelf.

# MATH CIRCLES WORK SHEET

**Name the Math Problem:** _____

**Explain the Problem:**

In your own words, explain what the problem is.

**Tackle the Problem:**

Provide a strategy that may help to solve the problem. Explain how you would use the strategy.

**Work the Problem:**

Use the space to work out the problem. Share your work with others (use the back of the sheet, if necessary).

**Answer the Problem:**

In your own words, provide a solution to the problem.

# POETRY CIRCLES

Poetry Circles are similar to Literature Circles in that they deal with words. Time spent working in a Poetry Circle is generally shorter, simply because poetry is usually not as long as a short story or novel. Poems evoke different emotions, thoughts, and images in fewer words. Discussing poetry allows students to see how different people react.

Have students select a poem to read on their own. At the same time, they can record everything on the role sheet for poetry. Once each member of the group has completed the sheet, the group can assemble to start the discussion. Each member should share his or her work sheet with the group. We find it works best if all students in the group share their word search results best, before moving on to images, meaning, and feelings they had after reading the poem.

We have included the work sheet for Poetry Circles, and two poems so you can try Poetry Circles with your class. Have fun!

# POETRY CIRCLES WORK SHEET

**Poem's Title:** _____

**Poem's Author:** _____

**Wonderful Word Search:**

Find 3 - 5 words that you think are wonderful in the poem. Explain why you think they are wonderful.

**Feeler:**

Describe your emotions—how the poem makes you feel. Prepare to share.

**Meaning Maker:**

Explain what the poem means to you.

**Image Maker:**

Create an image that comes to mind when you are reading the poem. (Be prepared to explain your image.)

## Life Is Tough...as a Pencil

Well, what are you waiting for?
I'm sharp, I'm pointy
I'm in a starting mode
So start pushing me around
loop de loops
swirly, swirls
Up, and down, back and forth
there I go

Wait! Don't push so hard
What do you think?
Harder does not make faster!
Oh, Oh I'm telling you so
Not that hard!
SNAP!

I could have told you so
Now back to that gizmo
It will gnaw me away
And now another attempt
Here we go
Elevate, and then down
back and forth we go again.
Turn me upside down
Rub, rub, push, push
A little blow and my pieces
Are swept away from the page

I'm telling You
Life is tough
As a pencil

## Life Is Tough...as a Writer

I'm ready to write
My pencil is sharp
the mind is keen
the paper is pristine
Now all I need
is the idea

Now I will not just sit and wait
Just start writing I must say
Let the words flow upon the paper
Here they come
Here they emerge
Wait, they're slowing down
A blockage!
A dam!
Don't give in, harder
Harder, Write!
Before the mind goes blank
Harder—
DRAT!

A broken pencil to interrupt
the concentration
Time to sharpen it
What a distraction!
Now where was I?
No, no that's not right.

Erase, erase, wipe away
the mistakes
My ideas are gone now
I'm telling you
Life is tough
As a writer

—Dave Leochko

# The Fly and I

Mountains of meatballs
A forest of broccoli
All placed before me
It's supper time I see.

There's nothing quite like
that first landing
On that tantalizing food
Ohhhh how the aroma draws me
No matter where I am
I know it's supper time.

The sound of the clanging plate
The tingle of the cutlery
I know it's supper time.

But for all the joy
One must be wary
For it is a most dangerous
time indeed
Yes, it is supper time.

Swishing, flapping, flailing hands
Ready to squish, flatten and stomp
Oh how would it be to have
Supper in peace
Just one time.

The cooking is done
The food is ready
The table is set
It's time to eat.

After all the precise preparation
There now sits before me
The savory smells
Mouthwatering meatballs
Crunchy, tasty broccoli
It's time to eat.

AND THEN IT HAPPENS!

Buzzing and humming
Pesky little critters
No matter how many swings
You take at it
He keeps coming back
Ready to land his dirty little feet
Right on top of my gourmet treat.

One hand on the fork
The other ready to swat
Oh how it would be
To eat in peace
Just one time.

—Dave Leochko

# Art Circles

People interpret art in different ways. Learning to appreciate art is an important part of a child's education. Art Circles give students opportunities to reflect on their own ideas about art and to hear different interpretations.

Have students work independently at first. Give the class a piece of art to look at. Each student should fill in the work sheet. Remind them to record the artist's name and the name of the piece. They can then describe the art in their own words. This can be very difficult, but it is good practice for descriptive writing.

On the work sheet, have students record their feelings (emotions) about the artwork. Also, have the students record what they think the artist istrying to say. (Recording their thoughts before the group comes together means they cannot change their mind to follow the opinions of others.) When the group assembles, students are mainly interested in what others felt when they looked at the art. They often talk about whether the artist's message is clear and what it means.

The group should come together once everyone has completed their work sheet.

# ART CIRCLES WORK SHEET

Artist's name: _____

Title of Piece: _____

**Describer:**

In your words, describe all that you see in the art.

**Feeler:**

Tell what feelings and emotions you have when you look at the art.

**Thinker:**

What do you think of the art? Give your opinions.

**Messenger:**

In your own opinion, what is the artist's message? What is the artist trying to communicate?

# Music Circles

In a Music Circle, we have students focus their attention on their reactions to music. Music can inspire feelings of joy or sadness, and much more. There are many different kinds of music, all of which evoke different emotions in different people. Music reminds us of events and people from the past, and so talking about music and how it affects us can be fun and interesting for students.

In Music Circles, students listen to and reflect on certain pieces of music. All types of music (jazz, country, classical, rap, hiphop, rock, pop, world music) work well.

To begin, play the piece for the class, then give students time to reflect on their own. Distribute the work sheet, and have the students record the feelings they have while listening to the music. Students can also describe what the message in the music might be. If the song has lyrics, have the students analyze what is said. Students can often express what they feel more easily by creating an image or picture that fits the music.

Once the students have finished their work sheets, they come together in their pre-assigned groups to discuss their responses. This type of exercise is interesting for students because there are often several different interpretations of the same music within one group.

We encourage students to express opinions about what they hear—to explain their preferences and back it up with solid reasoning, not saying simply that they like or do not like a piece of music.

# MUSIC CIRCLES ROLE SHEET

**Title of Music:** _____

**Artist:** _____

**Labeler:**

As you listen to the piece of music, record all the words that come to mind about the music.

**Feeler:**

Record how the music makes you feel (your emotions).

**Meaning Maker:**

What kind of message do you get from the music? If there are lyrics, what do you think they mean?

**Image Maker:**

As you listen to the music, create an image (drawing, diagram, doodle, etc.) that you think fits the music.

**Final Opinion:**

Do you like or dislike the piece of music? State your reasons.

# Bibliography

## Literature Circles Resource Books

Campbell Hill, Bonnie, Nancy Johnson, and Katherine L. Schlick Noe. *Literature Circles and Response.* Norwood, MA: Christopher-Gordon, 1995.

Daniels, Harvey. *Literature Circles—Voice and Choice in the Student-Centered Classroom.* York, ME: Stenhouse, 1994.

Schlick Noe, Katherine, and Nancy Johnson. *Getting Started with Literature Circles.* Norwood, MA: Christopher-Gordon, 1999.

## Literature Circles Resource Center Web Site

http://fac-staff.seatleu.edu/kschlnoe/LitCircles/